Catholic Lives

To Suha and Rachel

Catholic Lives

Contemporary Spiritual Journeys

GREG WATTS

GRACEWING

First published in 2001

Gracewing
2 Southern Avenue, Leominster
Herefordshire HR6 0QF

Cover picture: *Sheltered by Christ's Glory* by Elizabeth Wang © Radiant Light 2001 – www.radiantlight.org.uk

ISBN 0 85244 540 7

Typeset by Action Publishing Technology Ltd,
Gloucester GL1 5SR

Printed by MPG Books Ltd,
Bodmin PL31 1EG

Contents

Acknowledgements vii
Foreword *by Fr Michael Seed* ix
Introduction 1

The Web Designer 5
The Ballet Director 18
The Head Teacher 27
The Friar 38
The Tycoon 49
The Marxist Historian 56
The Artist 64
The Political Journalist 77
The Philosopher 86
The Student 100
The Social Activist 107
The National Front Member 119
The Scientist 130
The Politician 136
The Gangster 143

The Adoptee 151

The Traveller 160

The Counsellor 165

The Mother 175

The Undertaker 187

Acknowledgements

One night in November 1999 I made my way down into the crypt at St Ethelreda's church, Ely Place, London, for the launch of Dwight Longenecker's first book *The Path to Rome: Modern Journeys to the Catholic Church*. I didn't imagine that a few months later I would be beginning work on a follow-up book, my first also. That this happened is largely thanks to Dwight, who had been asked by Tom Longford to undertake the task himself. He was too busy with other projects, so he generously suggested that I offer to write a follow-up. And I am grateful to Tom for commissioning me to write *Catholic Tales*. I wish to thank all those in the book who agreed to share their faith journeys with me. I would like to thank all those who have helped in the researching and writing of this book, namely Fr Ben Kiely, Fr Michael Seed SA, James Parker, Debbie Bhati, Fr Cormac Rigby, Stratford Caldecott of the Centre for Faith and Culture, Oxford, Sister Sarah O'Dwyer, Clare Ward at Youth 2000, Fr Stephen Wang, Nick Baty and the Duke's Head Hotel in King's Lynn. In addition thanks go to the Catholic Missionary Society and Kevin Flaherty, editor of the *Catholic Times*, both of whom, by commissioning profiles from me, are partly responsible for the style of *Catholic Lives*. I also wish to thank John Lawson, Ev Scott and Lara Boyle for their constant friendship and encouragement during my career as a journalist and writer. However, had it not been for the staff at Campion House College, Osterley, particularly Jim Smith, the late Fr John Hughes SJ and Fr Denis Blackledge SJ, I might never have made a career in journalism. A special thanks must go to Saxon Bashford for his suggestions and advice, as well as his friendship. Finally, I wish to acknowledge my daughter Suha and my late daughter Rachel, who, with their uncomplicated faith and child-like trust, have not only brought me joy but also illuminated my own spiritual journey over the last ten years.

Greg Watts
Bermondsey, London

Foreword

by Fr Michael Seed

The term convert is used to describe anyone who has become a Catholic. But this is inaccurate as it really means a total rebirth, it means someone who desires baptism. But we use it as shorthand to describe a person who is received into full communion with the Roman Catholic Church.

The word convert has a sad connotation for a baptised Christian who becomes a Roman Catholic. It gives the impression that it's a new beginning when, in fact, it's a continuity of our Christian pilgrimage. The Catholic Church has a unique beginning 2000 years ago with the command of Christ to Peter and the apostles. It is the source of Christianity, and so, in a sense, to become a Catholic is a coming home.

For those who are not baptised the term convert is appropriate. For those of other faiths we have to be very sensitive. For example, when it comes to our brothers and sisters of the Jewish faith, we are very conscious that Christ was a Jew, as were his mother and his first followers. On the two occasions I have baptised a person of the Jewish faith I found it very nerve wracking. There is something inside me that would rather not do it out of respect for the tradition that is there. On both occasions the two people felt at home and more Jewish. And the longer I live the more Jewish I feel. When I go to services in synagogues

– Orthodox, Liberal, Progressive – I remind myself that this is what Jesus would have done, and I feel more Jewish. I am convinced that the Church often does God's worrying when God is able to do His own worrying. So when I ask myself does the Catholic Church have a monopoly on salvation I have to admit I don't know. I don't think so. I think it has a unique role in leading people to a knowledge of God, His love and the life of the Trinity. It is a beacon of hope for everyone. Christ is either who he said he was or he isn't.

It's always impressed me when the Pope gives his *Urbi et Orbi* message from the balcony of St Peter's in Rome at Christmas or Easter. He addresses the whole world. And that is the meaning of being Catholic. Catholicism embraces everything. In a sense, all of creation. All of creation is in the care of the Pope. All of creation is in the care of Christ. Catholicism is attractive because it's not exclusive or sectarian.

Jews, Muslims and Christians are all people of the book. We share the same prophets and belief in one God. When we look to other faiths – Sikhism, Hinduism, Buddhism – they all teach us something of the divine. They teach us about prayer, meditation and holiness. So when people feel prompted by God to continue their pilgrimage as Catholics they bring with them their traditions and gifts. Clearly there are certain things that have to be left behind. I once read that Goebbels was alleged to have based a lot of his SS methods on the Jesuits with whom he was training at one time.

With regard to my own journey of faith, I had been baptised and confirmed a Catholic by my birth mother, who handed me over to the Catholic Children's Society in Salford when I was about six months old. The Seeds, who adopted me, had also been Catholic. My adopted parents had both died by the time I was ten and my grandmother had brought me up. She was a holy woman and was in the Salvation Army. She said her morning and evening prayer, used to play evangelical singers of the 1940s, 1950s and 1960s and listen to Billy Graham on the radio. Then I became what was known as a Strict and Particular Baptist and I was going to become a minister of that tradition. I used to wander around outside football grounds handing out Bible tracts to convert the crowds. At eighteen I was confirmed in the Church of England.

But one night shortly afterwards, I went into a Catholic church in Bolton. Initially, I found it very dull and I thought the priest was a fogey and his sermon boring. It was a Latin Mass, so he had his back to the people. I could smell both incense and alcohol in equal measure. Many there had come out of the pub next door. But something said to me, 'This is normal.' The pews contained both sinners and saints and people of all backgrounds. Anyone could come in. Yet I had considered Catholics a sect and linked to the devil. I had thought they were beyond redemption.

The reason I became a Catholic and the reason I stay a Catholic are very different. I became one because of the dirtiness and sinfulness; the Catholic Church is able to cope with all of that very well. It's sublime. It's saintliness and despair, good and evil – it's the Church, the whole hodgepodge of humanity. It's very similar to the theology of Teilhard de Chardin, which is all about the consecration of the whole universe, the whole of creation. The essence of the Catholic Church – its substance, its foundation – is that it's the Christian Church. That's what I believe in.

But at the end of the day we are a bit like St Thomas Aquinas. After writing all his volumes of work he concluded that it was all straw. We live, we die, we do not have all the answers. We have to put everything in God's hands. We call this faith. And when we move by faith we live and if we don't we start to die. The Church's obligation is always to pick us up when we fall down; to encourage us. All of us can begin our day with faith and end our day with no faith. Even in the course of an hour we can move from faith to desolation.

I am still a Salvationist. I am still a Strict and Particular

Baptist. I am still an Anglican. I bring with me the love of preaching, the Bible and the evangelical zeal I encountered in those traditions. But I have to leave the exclusivity behind; the idea that we are saved, you are not.

The late Fr Feeney, a Jesuit in Boston, was excommunicated in 1953 because he said that outside the Roman Catholic Church there is no salvation. He repented before he died and the excommunication was lifted. Yet interestingly, Fr Avery Dulles, one of the professors who taught me at the Catholic University of America in Washington DC, left Presbyterianism for the Catholic Church through the preaching of Fr Feeney. So good can come out of what I would prefer to call eccentricity. Fr Feeney's preaching actually brought into the Church one of the great minds of this century.

So we bring with us all the good stuff but we have to work a little bit on our eccentricity and odd side. We need to put a lot of our baggage down. We need to change. And to live is to change often. We shouldn't be triumphalistic. We rejoice quietly that people have chosen to continue their journey in the Catholic Church. We don't give them medals – unless they are Miraculous Medals!

Fr Michael Seed is a Franciscan Friar of the Atonement and based at Westminster Cathedral, where he is ecumenical officer to Archbishop Cormac Murphy O'Connor.

Introduction

by Greg Watts

Had I not been baptised and brought up a Catholic by my parents, would I have ever made a decision to become a Catholic? This is a question I find myself unable to answer. I would hope so. But who can say.

I have always been intrigued by what leads some people to seek reception into the Catholic Church. Why? When were the seeds sown? By whom? Was it more of a head or more of a heart decision? How difficult was it? What was the process involved?

This book attempts to explore these questions, and others, with twenty Catholics from diverse backgrounds. Some had been a committed member of another Christian tradition, some had embraced another world faith, others had an ill-defined belief in some sort of a God, but would not have considered themselves religious. I hope it provides some interesting and revealing insights into both their faith and their lives. All are 'converts' apart from John Pridmore and Josie Callaghan. John was baptised Catholic but was not nurtured in the faith. Josie, on the other hand, came later in life to a much deeper, and radical, understanding of the faith she had grown up in. I have included their stories to underline the point that even if we are baptised a Catholic, or brought up a Catholic, we too are called to make a commitment at some stage in our life, and if we fall away (and some of us may do that often), a recommitment.

The central theme running through this book is that of a spiritual journey. Cardinal Hume liked to talk about us all being pilgrims on earth. This book has come out of my own spiritual journey and my travels and encounters over the last twelve years as a religious affairs journalist. I remember once interviewing Fr Peter Wilson of the Catholic Missionary Society, himself a convert, and he jokingly defined Catholicism as 'long haul religion'. That seems a perfect description.

Another recurring theme amongst those interviewed is one of coming home. For me, despite the struggles, doubts, sins and lukewarmness that have been features in my own spiritual landscape over the years, the Catholic Church has always felt like home. It has never occurred to me to join another church. Equally, New Age spirituality or that of so-called Eastern religions have failed to seduce me. For all its imperfections – and second collections – the Catholic Church is home. I have always seen it as a hospital for sinners rather than, as some would suggest, an exclusive international club. For me, the parable of the prodigal son best encapsulates the image of the Church. The Catholic Church, I believe, provides a sort of AA road map as we travel through life towards – we hope – Heaven.

This feeling of being at home has particularly struck me on my travels overseas. I remember, for example, in the summer of 1999 having breakfast one swelteringly hot morning with a parish priest at his church in the centre of Baghdad, and thinking here I was in a completely different culture, thousands of miles away from Britain, and, although we were divided by language and customs, we were united by a common faith. I have had similar feelings walking in the candlelit procession in Lourdes, praying in the basilica in Nazareth, attending Mass early one morning in a medieval church on a hill overlooking Budapest, and mingling with the pilgrims in St Peter's in Rome. Some Catholics bemoan the loss of Latin as a unifying factor in the Church, at least in the West. I have never held this view. What unites us is something much deeper than whether Mass is celebrated in a universal language. This is a point that James Parker makes in his story.

Despite the indifference and, occasionally, hostility exhibited towards the Catholic Church by some, particularly in certain sections of the media, the fact remains that up and down the country at any given time there are men and women seeking answers to the big questions and moving towards reception into the Catholic Church. It might be the person sitting next to you on the bus or behind you in the check out queue at your local supermarket. True, church attendances have been falling alarmingly in recent years, and some people find New Age ideas, or their local health club, more attractive and relevant than Christianity. However, long after New Age ideas have been discarded on the cultural rubbish dump, and the health clubs have closed down, the Church, despite crises, scandals, inquisitions, controversies and persecutions during its 2000 year history, will still be here, assuming the planet is still here, of course. We hear a lot of talk about people today being interested in spirituality rather than religion. But religion is simply organised spirituality.

What I found fascinating when I carried out the interviews was the variety of routes, signposts, resting places, and junctions that marked each individual journey of faith. Very often insignificant, or chance, incidents and encounters became turning points. This was the case for Alexis Pottinger when she reluctantly entered a Catholic church in Jamaica. For others, such as Kate Johnson, a personal crisis triggered the flowering of faith. Conrad Black's decision to be received into the Catholic Church came after a rigorous intellectual inquiry. For David Bintley it was the rich symbolism of the liturgy that drew him in; not celebrated in some magnificent cathedral, but in an ordinary church in Huddersfield. Reading G. K. Chesterton while in prison forced Joseph Pearce to examine Catholicism seriously and turn his back on the National Front.

Finally, what unfolds in these stories is the work of the Holy Spirit, unseen and unpredictable, but present in all the moments of our lives as we journey towards God. And like those bewildered and puzzled apostles 2000 years ago who encountered the stranger on their journey from Jerusalem, we too are walking along the road to Emmaus.

The Web Designer

As the train sped through south-east London, gazing out of the window at the back gardens, fleeting glimpses of high streets, modern factory units, church steeples and patches of greenery, I wondered what sort of woman Alexis Pottinger would turn out to be. I had been intrigued by her CV, as much by the gaps as the references to teaching, quilting in Jamaica, designing the web site for Westminster Cathedral and, now, the position of vocational training manager at the trendy sounding Hoxton Bibliotech. There was no mention of her family, but I knew that she had journeyed to Catholicism from Judaism. That was why I was on my way to interview her.

When I arrive at her flat in a secluded street, down the hill from Crystal Palace station, I am met by a bespectacled woman in her fifties. Her short hair is combed forward into a fringe and she is casually dressed in a blue top and jeans. She's apologetic for not contacting me sooner after I had first phoned her to ask if she would agree to be included in the book. Her father had died, aged eighty-six, she reveals in a well spoken voice. 'In fact, his obituary's in *The Times* today,' she adds modestly, sitting down in a wicker rocking chair and pointing to a photocopy of the article neatly placed on the table.

The obituary of her father is headed 'Barry Fealdman: Quiet and persistent patron of Anglo-Jewish art.' It goes on to reveal that he brought Anglo-Jewish artists and sculptors from the fringes into the mainstream of British art. This achievement was especially remarkable, the obituary goes on, because he had no training as either an artist or an art historian. He had educated himself by visiting as many museums as he could while serving with the Eighth Army during their conquest of Italy. I had glanced at his obituary in a copy of *The Times* left behind on a seat on the train. But I had no reason to connect it with Alexis.

Her living room has an air about it of someone who is disciplined, meticulous and artistic. A variety of pictures and art work, including an icon of Christo Pancreator and the original of the photo of her father – bearded, studiously sitting behind a typewriter – that had appeared in *The Times*. A few books stand on a shelf. The only one I can make out is a copy of *Early Christian and Byzantine Art*.

She's only just moved here, from Streatham, she says, placing a glass of orange juice in front of me, then adding with a grin that, technically, she's in Penge but Crystal Palace sounds more romantic. So what was her father like? I begin. From the obituary, he sounds a very strong and determined character.

He was, she nods vigorously, and then in her precise carefully modulated voice begins to recount her childhood in London.

Bohemian society and Judaism were the two dominant influences in her childhood, which was, she says, extremely happy and stimulating for her and her brother. 'It was a Jewish intellectual environment in the middle of London. From the age of three to twelve we were living above an art gallery and cultural centre in Portman Street. There were classical music concerts, choirs, drama, and poetry readings from those sixties poets such as Michael Horowitz. I used to help out serving coffee and tea.

'Both my parents came from Russian Jewish immigrants. My father came from an intellectual background, while my mother was from more of a peasant background. My father's parents settled in Liverpool, my mother's in the East End of London. My mother came from a huge family, most of whom lived in London, so we used to have these great family gatherings on occasions such as weddings and bar mitzvahs. On a Sunday we would catch the bus up to my grandmother's in Hackney, where we would meet up with various cousins. My parents were Reform Jews, though they had both been brought up as Orthodox. My father's father was a very strict Orthodox. He had a shop in Liverpool, which he used to close on a Saturday and, of course, lost a lot of business by doing that. In fact, he wanted my father to become a rabbi. But for economic reasons that wasn't possible. Interestingly, my mother used to work in computers in the very early days when they used to use punch cards. She worked for a company that did market research and her job was to punch holes in cards, which were then fed into a computer.'

So how strong was her religious upbringing? 'I started going to Hebrew classes at the age of three and my parents attended the West London Reform Synagogue on a regular basis. My father taught Hebrew there for twenty-five years. We carried on all the Jewish traditions such as the Friday night blessing of bread and wine and celebrating all the major Jewish festivals throughout the year.'

She developed an early interest in art, no doubt inspired by her father, and used to enter the annual art competition at the gallery. However, her father, aware of the struggles of artists, discouraged her from a career in art, advising her to treat it as a hobby. Pointing to a colourful pen and ink drawing on the wall, which she explains is a mask made up of birds and fishes, she tells me it was painted by Glasgow artist Scottie Wilson, who used to bring her a pack of marzipan balls when he visited the gallery. 'He was one of the artists I remember most. He was such a gentle, wise old man, who was once commissioned by Wedgwood to design a dinner service.'

She attended a Church of England primary school, where she had to go to church every week. 'I remember the church used to have a large crucifix, like you would find in a Catholic church, and it used to enthral me as I sat there during the service. I really felt Christ suffering on the cross, even at that age. I can recall going home one day and drawing a picture of Christ on the cross when I was about eight years old. But because I couldn't bear the thought of the nails I drew ropes instead. I showed it to my father and he was absolutely furious. He snatched it away from me and stopped me going to church any more. This was quite a momentous event in my early life. But because I loved my father so much I just dismissed any thoughts of Christ and Christianity from my mind.'

Her family moved to Maida Vale and she continued her education at a Church of England grammar school in Shepherds Bush. But here she attended separate Jewish classes and was excused from daily assembly. By the age of fifteen, after her bar mitzvah, and with the 'God is dead' movement gaining influence, even amongst some theologians, she says she lost her faith. 'All my friends were either atheists or agnostics except for one Catholic girl, which is very interesting.'

Believing that politics rather than religion seemed to hold the answers to the big questions of life, Alexis joined the Young Socialists and became heavily involved in their meetings and activities. 'As a teenager you have these ideals and you want to change the world, and I felt politics was the way to do this. Doing canvassing meant that we went to some of the poorest parts of London. And this had an effect on me because it was the first time I had seen people living in such terrible conditions. I felt that something had to be done about this. So I decided to study politics, thinking that maybe afterwards I would even go into a political career.'

Her desire to change the world led her to the University of Bristol. The late sixties were a time of unbridled liberalism, protests and sit-ins as the tide of anti-institutionalism, accompanied by slogans such as 'make love, not war', swept through university campuses in Europe and America. She says it was a tremendously exciting time, full of optimism and possibilities. But her attraction to politics as an agent of social and personal change evaporated when one day she overheard a sociologist, an economist and a psychologist planning the strategy for a sit-in.

'I heard them discussing crowd manipulation. I was totally shocked by this. And I thought, "Surely this won't work. Intelligent university students won't fall for this." But they did. Seeing this manipulation, I felt that this wasn't right and that if this was what politics was about, then I didn't want anything to do with it.'

Having lost faith in both Judaism and politics, she felt a vacuum in her life. So where next for answers to life? Catholicism, which was dealing with its own revolution and protest movements, after the Second Vatican Council and the publication of *Humane Vitae*, never even seemed an option. Leaving the University of Bristol for the last time, in the summer of 1969, she and a friend decided to go to Morocco, attracted by its exotic nature and desert culture.

Here, sitting alone in the desert one afternoon, she says with a sense of wonder in her voice that she had a powerful experience of the presence of God. 'For the first time in my life I realised that God existed and he was the creator of everything. I felt that the highest thing humanity could do was to search for God and get to know Him. It gave me a totally new perspective on the world. God felt real, not an idea or just a word, but alive. This overpowering feeling lasted for between five and ten minutes and the memory of it was so vivid that it has stayed with me right up to this moment. This was a major turning point in my spiritual journey.'

She returned to England after her holiday in Morocco with a renewed desire to find the right path to God. 'I found a book on Buddhism in the house. My mother had an interest in Buddhist philosophy. Reading about the four noble truths and other ideas in Buddhism I felt that I had found the way to reach God. Soon after I saw a Buddhist monk being interviewed on TV. He was an Englishman who had trained as a Buddhist priest in Thailand. It turned out that he had a meditation centre in Hampstead. He seemed happy and content, so I thought this is the person I should follow and I began attending weekly meditation classes with him.'

She was then invited by some friends to visit a Tibetan centre in Scotland, where she met a Tibetan lama who, seeing that she was genuinely seeking truth and knowledge, took an interest in her and offered to teach her Tibetan meditation. After a few months she was herself teaching meditation to beginners. Had a flamboyant, charismatic Jamaican artist and jazz musician not walked into the centre one day, then Alexis' life might well have turned out very differently.

'Seeing him for the first time, I felt this was the guru I had been looking for. He would just take out his flute and play this fantastic music and speak poetry. I thought, "Gosh, what an amazing person." It transpired that he was a lapsed Catholic, but he still believed in God. He was the first person to introduce me to the New Testament.

'Although I had, of course, been aware of it, I had never actually sat down to read it. For me he was the bridge between Buddhism and Christianity. Every day we would read the New Testament together. This was the first chance I had to get to know Christ on an intellectual level.'

Back in London, they began to spend a lot of time together. Her parents, she admits, found it hard to accept her new boyfriend. Mixed race relationships were not as common then as now. What's more, of course, Phillip wasn't Jewish. Alexis landed an administrative job at the London School of Economics and then moved to the former Polytechnic of Central London. She continued with the Buddhist meditation, but her interest in Christianity had now been sparked, if not ignited.

Phillip's desire was to return to Jamaica. He had developed diabetes by this time and was quite ill. Alexis agreed to go with him and decided to train as a teacher at the University of London's Institute of Education, so that she would be able to get a job.

In 1978 they flew to Kingston. But after a year trying to adapt to the culture she told him she wanted to return to England. His diabetes worsened and, after three years in London, Alexis agreed to give Jamaica another try for his sake.

Phillip died in 1985, leaving behind not only Alexis but, by now, their two children. 'At this time we were living in a seaside town near Montego Bay. He had told me he wanted to buy a house in Kingston. So I had found a nice house and told him it was in Franklyn Town. He said that it was a good place to buy in as it was a nice area. But it turned out that he hadn't been there for twenty-six years. And the house was actually in the ghetto. When he last knew it it had been a middle-class area. For my children's sake, I decided to remain in Jamaica. I wanted them to have an experience of living in a black culture. I felt that from the point of their personal identity it was really important.'

With her two children, and no husband, she lived in the heart of the ghetto for the next ten years, listening to the sound of gun battles outside at night. She's clearly much tougher than she looks.

She leans forward slightly and begins moving her hands as she describes what became, for many reasons, an extraordinary period of her life. 'I was the only white person in the area. My children learned to be street wise and they survived. But I found it very difficult. I was totally isolated. The friends I had were scattered around Jamaica. They wouldn't come to my house because they thought it was too dangerous. We used to have curfews and you would see armoured cars going down the street. The police always walked around with automatic guns because of the gang warfare.' She adds that although she was burgled, which never really bothered her because she's never been that attached to material things, she was never subjected to violence.

She started a craftwork business, making quilted items, purses, cushions and bags, which were sold in craft shops.

Over time, she established a reputation as a talented quilter and then moved into designing costumes for Jamaican performers, including Rita Marley, wife of the legendary singer. In addition, she displayed her art quilts in a number of exhibitions on the island. Feeling drawn to some kind of community work, she set up projects to teach women, both in the ghetto and in the rural areas, business skills and the art of quilting. Later, in 1992 she took up a part-time post teaching creative quilting at the University of the West Indies in Mona. But life wasn't easy, bringing up two children alone, being very much an outsider, and having to make ends meet when the quilting was not going so well. Here, she says, she learnt the valuable lesson of what was really essential for survival: food, water, shelter and adequate clothing.

'I still saw myself as a Buddhist but felt that there was something missing in my life. I continued to read the Bible but I only saw Christ's teachings in an intellectual way. I'd been to a few churches but they hadn't really touched me. The thing about Jamaica is that everybody believes in God there. It's a very Christian culture. I once read that in Jamaica there are more churches per head of the population than anywhere else in the world. On Sundays everybody dresses up and goes to church. Being in the middle of this Christian culture was fascinating. Although I lived next to a Pentecostal church, and would hear the singing and clapping, which often seemed to go on for hours, I was never tempted to go in. I thought it was too emotional for me.'

One day a woman invited her to visit her church. Alexis agreed, more out of politeness and curiosity than anything else. 'When we arrived I was horrified to discover it was a Catholic church, Ss Peter and Paul. Jews are not very keen on Christianity, to say the least, and especially Catholicism. I really didn't want to go in. I was about to turn around and walk away when she beckoned from inside. I thought I can't be rude, so I went in. And the minute that Mass started it was like a thunderbolt had hit me. I felt,

"This is my spiritual home!" What really struck me was the similarity with a synagogue service. The reader processed in carrying the lectionary, which was similar to the way the scrolls are carried around the synagogue. And when it came to the blessing of the bread it reminded me of what my father used to do on a Friday night. And even the tunes sung by the cantor had a Jewish sound to them. I was overwhelmed and knew this was my spiritual home. I did not yet realise that it was Christ I had found, but I knew this was God's house.'

A few weeks later she was invited to the celebration to mark a feast day. 'I wasn't very well at the time and I hadn't been selling much of my work. I was quite hungry. In Jamaica there's no social security, so when you don't earn, you don't eat. And I had this wonderful meal. A spiritual and a physical healing took place on that day. I returned to the church the next week and told one of the Servite sisters that I wanted to become a Catholic. I joined the RCIA programme,' she says, then, her face rippling into a smile, adds 'As I was quite well known, mixed with Rastafarians and dressed Rasta-style with African prints and patchwork hats, they didn't quite know what to make of me.'

From the first day, she reveals, she knew she had a vocation in the Church. It was some time though before she realised what it was to be. Feeling that she needed something deeper than the RCIA programme, she spoke to the parish priest who introduced her to an American Jesuit for spiritual direction. 'He was the first person who accepted me totally as I was, took me from where I was and understood the level I was thinking on. I used to go to see him every week and we would have the most wonderful conversations. He'd been the director of the Jamaican Centre for Spiritual Development. He instructed me for the second year of my catechumenate, exploring Richard McBrien's book, *Catholicism*.

'The thing that always bothered me about Judaism was the exclusivity about it. I used to go to Jewish clubs as a teenager, but they were so cliquey and focused on the material side of Judaism. In Matthew's gospel Jesus says, "I haven't come to abolish the law. I have come to fulfil it." When I read Hebrews I came to understand this. Coming from a Jewish background it made a deep impression on me because it was written for a Jewish community. I have always felt very privileged to have come to Christ from a Jewish background because there is so much I grew up with that I see in the gospels and can relate to. He criticised the self-righteousness of Judaism and I had experienced this myself. I was coming from the same point as the disciples. And the other thing that really struck me about Christ's teaching was the call to love one's enemies. It was so totally radical for me.' So, have you ever been to Israel? She shakes her head. 'No. I'm waiting for the right time.'

Following her baptism, by immersion at dawn in July 1994 at the Church of the Holy Cross, she began to think about returning to London. After talking it through with the priests and nuns who had become friends, and who had given the kind of support she had missed for most of her time in Jamaica, she booked three tickets and was soon walking through arrivals at Heathrow Airport. She booked into a hotel in Victoria and sought advice about what to do from a priest at Westminster Cathedral. He recommended she registered with Westminster city council's homeless persons unit. But when she arrived for her interview she was informed that she was intentionally homeless because she had sold her house in Jamaica. So instead she rented a small flat in Stoke Newington. As she began looking at job vacancies, it became apparent that she needed to acquire some computer skills. She enrolled on a computer course in Hackney and, in order to get back into the swing of work, began helping out at The Passage Day Centre next to Westminster Cathedral. 'I got far more out of working at The Passage than the homeless people I helped. It gave me the discipline of getting up in the morning.' But life wasn't easy back in London, signing on at the DSS in Dalston, finding a school for her son and trying to find some work for herself.

She says that she was shocked at how secular and decadent Britain was. 'Jamaica is very conservative and sex is private. But in Britain sex was everywhere. In Jamaica if a woman was walking around and her petticoat was showing someone would point it out to her.'

Attending Mass in England also proved to be a bit of a cultural shock. 'Whereas in Jamaica, Mass was often accompanied by exuberant singing and the sign of peace could take ten minutes, in London the liturgy was much more restrained.'

She found a spiritual director, first a Jesuit at Southwell House and then a layman at Westminster Cathedral's centre for spirituality. So what is the value of having a spiritual director? 'I think it helps to see how God is moving in your life and listen to His voice. A spiritual director helps you to interpret your life spiritually and to maintain a spiritual perspective. Because your director sees you at intervals he can see developments. He might say, "When you came last time you were saying this, and how you're saying this. May be God is showing you this is the way go to." Often in the midst of day to day living you can't see all of this for yourself.'

As she was unemployed, she could choose from a variety of courses that were on offer in order to get back to work. Wanting to build on her creative skills, in 1996 she did a six-month course in desk top publishing followed by a course in web design at Hoxton Bibliotech. Information technology, she says, came easy to her, mainly because it called for the same kind of precision as quilting. She eventually landed a job as a lecturer at Hoxton Bibliotech and then, a few months later, was appointed vocational training manager, responsible for overseeing courses in web design and customer care, largely for those on low incomes.

So how did you get the job to design the web site for Westminster Cathedral and Cardinal Hume? I ask. That's quite an achievement. She gives a little laugh. 'Well, I went to the cathedral and asked one of the priests if the cathedral had a web site. He told me they didn't. So I collected all the information on the cathedral I could and began to work on a design.' Her work impressed the staff at the cathedral and they asked her to complete a similar project for Cardinal Hume.

While studying at the Hoxton Bibliotech, she used to go to daily Mass around the corner at St Monica's. There she became friendly with a woman who was a member of the Servite Secular Institute. 'When she explained what it meant, it suddenly dawned on me that this would be ideal for me. Being a widow with children, I couldn't go into a religious community. And when I went to my first meeting I felt so at home meeting women who shared the same values as me. I realised that I had been pretty much living the life of an institute member.'

Later she discovered the Servites had been founded in the thirteenth century by seven cloth merchants from Florence, one of whom, she adds with a twinkle, was St Alexis. In 1998 she began formation. She attends meetings every two months, usually in the form of away weekends, and studies the way of life of consecrated secularity, including the meaning of vows, the history and constitutions of the Institute, the Servite charism and the Rule of St Augustine, which the Servite order follows.

'Vows in a secular institute are just the same as in a religious congregation. You take temporary vows for three years, then renew them for two years. And then after five years you can take perpetual vows,' she explains.

But why does she feel the need to take vows? 'To consecrate one's life to God you have to have the support of other people. Trying to follow the path to holiness in the middle of a very secular society is not easy. I work in a new media company, which is about as secular as you can get. Without these regular meetings, which really nourish my spiritual life, I don't think I could do what I'm trying to do. I feel that God has called me to consecrate myself to

Him as a member of the Institute, and that this consecration will free me to serve Him as He wants me to.'

She talks with great enthusiasm about the Internet and the possibilities it opens for exchanging information and evangelisation. She carries out most of her correspondence by e-mail now. 'I feel my apostolate is bound up with the Internet. When I first heard about it I thought, "What a great tool for evangelisation." The Westminster Cathedral web site has a thousand hits a day. It allows people from all over the world to find out what's happening in the cathedral. There's information about the centre or spirituality, The Passage. And there's a whole music programme every month.' She adds that through her work in Hoxton she is evangelising, not explicitly but implicitly, by the way her Christian values permeate her work.

She nods when I suggest that this is undercover work and that the secular media today resembles the media in Eastern Europe under Communism in the way that Christianity is seen. So does she think evangelists should be sent into chat rooms? 'Possibly. I hadn't really thought about it. The Irish Jesuits have a web site called Sacred Space. In the middle of the day I sometimes log on to their web site and have a few moments of prayer.'

I remark that she has led, to say the least, a pretty unusual life. She has, she acknowledges with a smile. 'I think what happened when I was in Morocco was that I actually fell in love with God at that point. But because I had no Christian background and no concept of what consecrated life was I just carried on looking for a husband. If I'd known about the consecrated life I would probably have entered it then.'

The Ballet Director

'But what also hit me was the strangeness and power of that liturgy. It was like a different world to me. And I felt it was something I wanted to be part of.'

David Bintley, artistic director of the Birmingham Royal Ballet, is recounting his first time at Mass. It was the day after his wedding. His bride Jenny had not long returned to the Catholic Church after being lapsed for a number of years. When she suggested that he accompany her to St Patrick's in Huddersfield he agreed, not out of any deep spiritual yearning, he admits, but more because, well, they had just got married and Catholicism was important to her.

We are in his spacious and smart office at the Birmingham Royal Ballet in the heart of the city. He's a small, darting sort of man with an untidy mop of hair, dressed in a T-shirt and casual trousers. As he talks, moving his hands from side to side, he exudes an energy that draws you in to what he is saying.

All I knew about him was from an article I'd read in the *Daily Telegraph*, which described him as 'one of Britain's cleverest showmen' and said that he had turned down the directorship of the Royal Ballet. I decided to play safe and begin the interview with a few questions about his childhood.

He tells me he grew up in the Yorkshire village of Honley. Although his Yorkshire vowels have been diluted by his time in London, there's no mistaking his northern roots. Both his parents were musicians and music and, to a lesser extent, theatre shaped his early years at home. 'I got stage struck at a very young age, really as a consequence of the Sunday school concert I did,' he says, spooning sugar into my cup.

Neither the Methodist church, where he went to Sunday school, nor the Church of England primary and grammar schools left much of an impression on him in terms of faith, he concludes, shaking his head as if puzzled by the fact. 'In the Church of England schools I went to we had morning assembly, recited the Lord's Prayer and attended services at Christmas and Easter, but that was about it. And although my parents had been brought up in the Church of England, they weren't church goers and left me to make up my own mind.'

His childhood dream was to be a ballet dancer. 'I started dancing when I was eleven as a way to get on stage. But when I was fourteen I really got the ballet bug and all I wanted to do was get to the Royal Ballet School, which, I knew, was the best school in the country. Education sort of went a little by the board. But I did okay at school, even though I was travelling fifteen miles a day three days a week to attend ballet lessons and didn't get home some nights until midnight.'

So, did you get ribbed at school for being a ballet dancer? You know, the cliché image of lads in tights, that sort of thing. 'Yeah, a little bit. But my friends were fine. We just didn't talk about it. I didn't fit the stereotype. I got into fights and I was in the football and athletic teams,' he says with a shrug.

At sixteen he was offered a place at the Royal Ballet School, an unusual occurrence for a Yorkshire lad, he readily admits. Being creative usually meant joining a brass band, not going down to London to be a dancer. His parents were far from well off and had to scrimp and save to pay his fees for the two-year course. 'When you go to the Royal Ballet School you hope that when you leave you will get a job with the Royal Ballet or what was then Sadlers Wells Ballet. And I did, by the skin of my teeth.'

A serious knee injury soon after arriving at the Royal Ballet threatened his career as a dancer. But after a successful operation, he returned to his classes and, inspired by the likes of Margot Fonteyn, Rudolph Nureyev and Frederick Ashton, he left the school not only with the first prize in choreography but also a much sought after place at Sadlers Wells Royal Ballet, now Birmingham Royal Ballet. His career blossomed quickly and he soon found himself in leading roles, before being appointed resident choreographer. In 1986 he left Sadlers Wells to become resident choreographer at the Royal Opera House, Covent Garden. He decided to go freelance in 1993, and soon secured commissions from seven companies around the world. In 1995 he took up his post as artistic director at the Birmingham Royal Ballet.

While a student at Sadlers Wells he had met another dancer, Jenny. Eventually, they moved into a flat together and after a couple of years decided to get married. By now Jenny, who had come from a devout Catholic family, had returned to practising her faith. 'At that time, I wasn't religious at all. And as for Catholicism, it all seemed a bit like witchcraft to me,' he laughs.

Originally, he and Jenny were going to get married in London. But David had been distinctly unimpressed by the lifeless church he had visited around the corner from Sadlers Wells. So instead they decided to get married at the Anglican church in his home village of Honley.

His voice slows as he recalls that day in 1981. 'Jenny was three-quarters of an hour late in turning up. So I just had to sit waiting in the church. And it was freezing. The village was covered in snow. I had plenty of time to think, and I remember looking up at the stained glass window of the crucifixion, which I remembered well from the times when I had sung with the school choir in the church, and, looking at the image of Christ on the cross, I just thought to myself, "I don't believe any of this stuff. What on earth am I doing here? It's pointless." And to cap it all the vicar was standing there in his slippers, wondering where Jenny was.

'Then something inside me, as clear as a bell, said, "Yes, you do believe this." It was just like someone next to me had said it to me. And the tone was almost mocking. It was as if for such a long time I had believed but I'd denied it or gone against it.'

It was the day after, at St Patrick's, Huddersfield, that he went to Mass for the first time, and experienced the tremendous power of the Catholic liturgy even when celebrated not in some magnificent cathedral but in what he describes as a 'farmyard of a church', where the words of the priest were interrupted by the shrieks and howls of babies and toddlers.

'When we walked into the church I was knocked out because it was so full. I discovered that this was one of five Sunday Masses. There were old people, young people, children, babies. It was unlike what I had experienced before. The churches I'd been in had been empty, cold and as far removed from the message of Christ as you could possibly imagine. This, I thought to myself, is what a church should be like. It shouldn't be separate from life, but part of it.

'Not really having a backbone in the Church of England, which derives its liturgy from the Catholic Church, I'd never heard so many set things. All the different parts of the Mass – the readings, the offertory, the Eucharistic Prayer, the consecration – just seemed so rich to me. Not only this, they seemed mystical. And very un-English, which is what I like and what a lot of people in England don't like. My aunt, for instance, although she had been a very devout Anglican all her life, stopped going to church when they introduced the sign of the peace.'

He says he has continued to find the Mass a source of fascination and inspiration, what with its language, movement, symbolic use of colour, and changes that reflect seasons such as Lent, Easter and Advent. 'When I travel around the world with the company it's wonderful to be able to go to Mass in different countries and still understand what's happening, even though it's in another language. One Good Friday I attended Mass in a town in Brazil. I found the Latin American liturgy so powerful. They had a crucifix that was extraordinary! It was the most gory thing I had ever seen. Then on another occasion we were in Crete, where there was a resident Catholic priest but there was no Catholic church. But the Greek Orthodox Church allowed us to celebrate Mass in the garden of one of their churches, on the top of a hill. It was marvellous being there in the blazing sunshine with all these people from different parts of Europe. I felt there was a real sense of pilgrimage about this Mass, leaving my hotel room and going up that hill just to attend Mass. It was marvellous.'

Having had such a powerful experience in St Patrick's, he began going to Mass regularly when he returned to London, at St Melitus in Finsbury Park, and was soon facing what would have been unthinkable a few years before: that he wanted to become a Catholic. 'I just wanted to be received into the Church. I had begun to read a lot about Catholicism, although I didn't go about it in a very scientific way.' He adds when pressed that the two Christian writers he most enjoys are C. S. Lewis and Malcolm Muggeridge, both of whom, like himself, discovered Christianity later in life.

He began instruction with a young priest at St Melitus and then, when they moved the short distance to Stroud Green, with a priest at St Peter-in-Chains. He jokes that there seemed no rush to get him in. He was received into the Church during the Easter Vigil in 1984. A few years after he and Jenny remarried in a Catholic church.

Being artistic director of the Birmingham Royal Ballet means that he spends a large part of the year on tour in either the UK or overseas. And it can sometimes be 11 p.m. before he gets home to Jenny and their two sons, fifteen-year-old Michael and four-year-old Gabriel. So there is little opportunity to become as involved in his local Catholic parish and school as he was when he lived in north London.

So, did he find some Catholic doctrine and practices difficult? He shifts in his chair and looks thoughtful. 'My biggest jump was hearing that voice in the church at Honley. Sure, there are certain things in the Catholic Church that are easy to challenge intellectually. But for the most part I welcome the rules the Church has. I believe that if you start following your conscience, then unless you have some really deep rooted problem with some aspect of the faith, then you're just bending the rules to suit yourself. Change when it has to do with the eternal has to come slowly.'

I ask him how his friends and colleagues reacted to his new faith. He says that he had all the fervour traditionally associated with a convert and that some of those who knew wondered if he had lost his marbles. Recognising that not everyone might share his enthusiasm for the Church he learned to be more restrained in case he put people off.

Becoming animated, he argues that art has a vital role to play in communicating the Christian message. 'I'm an artist and I think that there are things you can do in certain mediums that you can't in a church. For example, Scorcese's film *The Last Temptation of Christ* is a very holy film. I know the Church was saying don't go and see it, but I can't believe a film like this can be blasphemous. It may challenge our view of Christ and it may throw up certain ideas which we reject immediately. But that whole sequence in the desert with Christ and the snake and the lion was superb. It was really poetic.' As he says the word 'poetic' a look of pure admiration spreads across his face.

The Church, of course, was at the centre of culture in the Middle Ages. Music, art, drama, dance, architecture and even the law took their inspiration from the Church and the Bible. Today, at least in Britain, Catholic artistic expression has been pushed to the margins. The highly popular exhibition Seeing Salvation, at London's National

Gallery, was a reminder of how great Christian art once was. David now notes with disdain that instead of the kind of works that someone like Michelangelo once produced we are given 'appalling stuff on piety stalls'.

Music, he observes, is one area where Christianity has continued to exercise a strong influence. He points out that the work of the composers James McMillan and John Tavener is firmly rooted in their Christian faith and vision of the world. However, he claims this is easier to do in music because the medium is not so literal and the subject matter can recede into the background.

He says he doesn't hide his faith in his work with the Birmingham Royal Ballet, but staging productions with explicit Christian stories and themes is difficult from a commercial point of view. 'The potential danger in my world is that when you present Biblical stories you always come up against people wearing long robes and sandals. And people are not going to watch that.'

Nevertheless, in 1998 he staged John Tavener's *Protecting Veil*, a work in which seven dancers portray the Virgin Mary at different stages of her life. 'It had everything, the Nativity, the Crucifixion, the Resurrection. And it was received in rapt silence by the audience. The extraordinary thing was how many people didn't know what was going on because they didn't know the story. As Christians, we shouldn't assume that everyone knows what we are talking about.' He then adds after a pause. 'I must admit though that I was quite surprised by the number of people who didn't know what was going on.

'The piece had a real gravitas. I don't know how it affected the audience but the atmosphere surrounding it was a very unusual one. I remember at the end of the first stage rehearsal when the seven women use their veils as tears to represent the tears of the Mother of God and the music fades away, it started to rain on the metal roof. All the girls on stage looked at each other in amazement and went, "Wow!" Sure, I know we get a lot of rain in this country but ... it was like a spell.

'But as much as I would like to do more work like that I know that there's going to be resistance. And there is a certain amount of pressure to stage successful work. So what I try to do is make all my work, especially if it's narrative, informed by my belief. I'm not saying it's Christian ballet but I go out of my way to make moral points, even if what I'm doing can often appear immoral.'

His production of *Arthur*, costing £500,000, was the largest ever created in Britain. Part I was shown in 2000 and Part II will be shown in 2001. To stage a ballet about King Arthur has been one of his ambitions for twenty years, he reveals. But while the story, part legend, part factual, took place hundreds of years ago, he took care to make sure that the message had a relevance for the twenty-first century. His decision to open the ballet with a rape was, however, one he only did after much soul searching, he reveals.

'I did this because I wanted to show the kind of violent and brutal society that Arthur was born into; the society that he changed. If I hadn't shown the rape scene, you wouldn't have had such a strong image of that society.'

The 1999 conflict in Kosovo was very much in his mind when he sat down to plan the ballet, he explains. 'The two most pertinent things that happened in the Balkans were the ethnic cleansing and the use of rape as a tool of war. I understand that the number of abortions in the region has gone up by something like 10,000% because of the number of women who were raped by either policemen or soldiers. If you're doing a hard hitting piece like this, a piece that is trying to say something about the truth, then you can't pretend it didn't happen.'

But isn't there a danger in, perhaps, unwittingly being sucked into the trend to use sex to sell seats? 'I have to think really deeply about the issues in a production. My depiction of sex and violence is always a negative one. There's always a consequence to these kinds of actions. But it's hard to get inside other people's heads. In some ways, I'm glad about those letters I got about that rape scene because from the outset I did want it to be a shocking thing.' He gives a long pause. 'But it's hard to achieve that effect now because we are so inured to it by the number of rapes we've seen in films.'

The Head Teacher

Janet Sheehan, head teacher at St Anne's Primary School, Whitechapel, pauses and says with feeling in her voice. 'I think it's a real strength of Catholic education, this community. You can't buy that.' She talks expansively, moving rapidly from one subject to another, the passion and sheer enjoyment of what she is doing shining through. 'I'm told that I'm very enthusiastic. I don't see it really. And I'm told I'm a very good saleswoman. But I couldn't sell something if I didn't believe in it.'

Through her office window I can see a group of children, in their blue uniforms, sitting with a teacher under the shade of a tree as a scorching June sun beats down. Taken as a snapshot, this could be a scene in some rural corner of England rather than in the heart of London's East End, just a few streets away from Whitechapel High Street, where the traffic groans and hoots relentlessly while a cosmopolitan array of people lingers amongst the market stalls, selling tea towels, alarm clocks, Barbie dolls and jeans. Around the corner is Brick Lane, where pungent smells of spices waft from numerous curry-houses, competing for the appetites and pockets of City suits, and late-night groceries sell strange-looking fish and exotic vegetables.

Janet enthuses about the area – 'vibrant', 'fascinating' – although she knows all too well about its reputation for crime, poverty and racial tensions. In the 1970s and 1980s the National Front staged a number of provocative demonstrations here. Whitechapel has been a transient and ethnically fluid area for many years, something well illustrated by the mosque in Brick Lane, which was formerly a synagogue and before that a French Huguenot church.

A well-built woman in her forties with sharp features and short fair hair, Janet is dressed in a long flowery skirt, yellow shirt and jacket. On the wall of her office are paintings by some of the children and a card that reads: 'Together towards excellence, with God as our guide.' Family and school photos are sprinkled here and there on shelves and work-tops. She's just returned from one of her MBWAs (management by walkabout).

As usual this morning, she had got out of bed at 6 a.m. at home in Woodford, checked her answerphone to see if any teachers had phoned in sick, breakfasted, showered and then driven along the A102(M) until she picked up the number 8 bus route at Old Ford and followed it to Bethnal Green. By 7.45 a.m. she was sitting at her desk studying the day's school diary, taking her first phone calls and checking her e-mails. At 8.30 a.m. the first parents were arriving for the breakfast club. Janet says she begins the day with a list and ends the day with a list, but with ten more things on it.

Although St Anne's has the capacity for 350 children in its nursery and school there are currently only 284 children on its roll, a number of whom have what Janet describes as 'significant special needs'. Over 50% of the children receive free school meals, which are an indicator of poverty. Janet is the fifth head since Ofsted inspectors concluded in 1996 that St Anne's had serious weaknesses.

This is all changing now, beams Janet, who is in a buoyant mood after the Ofsted inspection the previous week. 'The Ofsted registered inspector told me that we were outstanding in leadership,' she says with a glow of pride that is to be expected when you have achieved what many would have said was the impossible. 'It's fantastic. I didn't think the school would turn around so quickly.'

When I ask why this has happened she replies breezily it's due to vision and leadership. 'What's the quote? "Without a vision the people perish."' Vision, I learn during the interview, is a word that she likes to use a lot. 'I think the staff were ready to be led because they had had six head teachers. The chemistry just worked really. Problems had to be diagnosed – and there were weaknesses with the teaching – and consultants were brought in from outside. It's no good telling people you're not very good at something and then not doing anything about it. I think fundamental to it all was re-evaluating things and focusing on this new mission statement.' Pointing to a chart on the wall she says she wants to raise the current attendance level of 91% to 95%.

Janet talks repeatedly about the mission statement, which was one of the first things she put her mind to when she arrived at the school the previous September. She brought in leading Catholic educationalist Dr John Sullivan from St Mary's College, Strawberry Hill, to help her reverse the fortunes of the school. She's a woman who won't tolerate negativity or accept the view held by some that just because children live in an inner city area nothing much can be expected from them. The leafy suburbs are not problem free, she points out.

'When we began to think of revising our mission statement we had a training day. We had a meal, and a special Mass at St Anne's. It was one of those Masses where the hairs stand up on the back of your neck. And it was during the Mass that I felt that was the first time the team had gelled together with me. The enthusing with the vision part wasn't that hard. I've been fairly pro-active. But rhetoric has to match reality. I'm constantly holding up the mission statement to scrutiny. I had a child this morning who was very rude. I asked him, "Where in our mission statement does it say that?" I could take any child and ask, "What's our mission statement?" And they could tell me. And so could the staff. You have to live it. You have to walk the walk and talk the talk. And sometimes I fail. When we get the report in about six weeks it will say something like, "The vision of the key staff is outstanding." When the registered inspector fed back to us he talked about everybody singing from the same hymn sheet. We put the Catholic ethos into practice by being welcoming, friendly and open.'

Given that St Anne's is located in an area with a high Bengali population, it has not gone unnoticed by the Ofsted inspectors that there are only two Bengali children on its roll, although between them pupils have fifteen different first languages.

Janet candidly admits there is prejudice amongst the parent body and she knows she has to walk a very difficult line in addressing this, as the school is, she suggests, the only contact many parents have with the Church. 'Some parents are frightened that I am trying to turn this school into a Bengali school. But we are trying to break down this kind of culture. I meet regularly with the head teacher at Thomas Buxton Junior, which is 100% Bengali. And that's good for my children to see me going over there and vice versa. There's a drama project coming up soon which will involve children from St Anne's going to Thomas Buxton.'

Nevertheless the absence of Bengali pupils at St Anne's cannot simply be put down to racial prejudice, she adds. 'Bengali parents don't want to send their children to a school where they will be in a minority. Why would they when there is a school over the road that is 100% Bengali?'

So how does she get parents to share her vision and become involved in the life of the school? 'Mainly through personal contact. I have an open door policy. If a parent asks me if I have a minute I always try to find one. I produce a weekly newsletter, which the Ofsted inspector loved.'

Responding to results from a questionnaire that was sent to parents she changed parents' meetings from the evenings to the mornings. 'I wouldn't say I've cracked it yet. Parents are going to take longer than the staff to trust me. When parents come into the school they are often revisiting their own school days. And if you were educated in the 1950s, as I was, when the cane was around, you might have had bad experiences.'

She becomes uncharacteristically crestfallen and confides that a few days before she had had her worst interview ever with a parent, who had accused her of being rude and aggressive. She admits that it still hurts 'because you like to feel you're pleasing everybody. I apologised and said I was sorry. If I can't do that, how can I expect anyone else to do it?'

So who inspired her? 'It was in my blood. Apparently, I used to have assemblies with my grandparents and they had to pretend they were at school.' She pulls a face and laughs. 'Dreadful! I never wanted to be anything else but a teacher.'

She was born in Derbyshire. Her parents had met while they were both teaching at Swanwick Hall Grammar, which is now a well-known conference centre. When she was eight the family moved to Ormskirk, Lancashire, where Janet was sent to a Church of England school, which she hated.

'It was everything I now don't believe in. You sat in numbered seats in classes of about fifty. I sat in the back right-hand corner and the bottom child was up by the teacher's desk. Every week you had a test and every month you moved around. But I really hated it because of school dinners. One of my teachers was the deputy and his job was to cane the naughty boys after playtime. I was absolutely traumatised by this. It was the complete opposite of what I want my school to be.'

Ormskirk Grammar School, where her father was Head of Geography, provided a more positive experience. She became head girl and emerged with nine O levels and three A levels. 'It was a good school but the teaching was old fashioned compared to what it is now.' She'd been musical from an early age and eventually went on to play the flute in the Southport Youth Orchestra. 'I think of myself as someone who is musical but not very good at it.'

Her father was a Welsh Presbyterian and her mother a Scottish Presbyterian. Catholics – or 'Papists', as her father described them – were a bit of a mystery to Janet. Because there was no local Presbyterian church, Janet was baptised a Baptist. Later on, at one point, she was simultaneously attending a Congregational church and a Methodist youth club. 'Although Lancashire is quite a strong Catholic area, I hardly knew any Catholics. They were educated totally separately at St Bede's High School. There was no animosity. We just moved in different circles.'

Her childhood was extremely happy, she says, delight written on her face at the recollection of it. 'I was made to feel very important. I was loved, I was valued, all the things that you would want for a child. One thing my mother taught me was to laugh until you cried. With my dad being a geographer and my mum being a historian we often used to go out to visit historical houses and different places. One of my earliest memories from my childhood in Derbyshire is being taken to Crich to see the fossils and going to the ice cream shop in the village. I always felt – and still feel it – that I had to succeed. It was very important that I succeeded to please my parents. But I think that's typical of older children, isn't it?'

Leaving school in 1969, she says, you either went to university, training college, or into nursing or banking. She went to the University of London's Queen Mary College, where she gained a degree in geography, and then spent a year at the Institute of Education to obtain her PGCE.

In 1973 she was taken on at Woodford County High School and spent the next ten years there. During this time she met her husband, Patrick, and they married in 1981. 'I remember one of the first times I went out with my husband. He took me to La Salette working men's club in Dagenham. This was a real culture shock. And there on what seemed to be a dais of blue carpet was the priest, sitting with a cigar and a whisky! I was horrified! I thought, "My God, there's a priest. He's drinking, he's smoking and he's in a pub." My father comes from a tradition where they have dry weddings.'

Meeting Patrick turned out to be a major spiritual junction in her life. 'My husband is the beginning of my journey of faith towards Catholicism. He was a cradle Catholic but had lapsed. The play *Once a Catholic Always a Catholic* had great resonance for him. He comes from a lovely Irish family. Vatican II wouldn't be a term he would use, but he always says he can remember the day the nuns stopped hitting him and then began playing guitars.

'When his mother became seriously ill, Patrick made her promise that she would stay alive to see his first child born. And on the day of the birth she died. So he had the bitter sweet experience of the death of someone he adored and his first born. He started going back to Church at this time and I went with him. It seemed the right thing to do. We just needed to do it.'

By the late 1980s they had three children running around the house and Janet was having to examine schools from the other side of the fence. 'We had to make a decision about which school they should go to. I went to see Angela Myler, the head at St Antony's, the local Catholic primary school, and explained that my husband was a Catholic, but I wasn't. "Oh, they must have a Catholic education," she said immediately.'

By now Catholicism had begun to intrigue her and she was curious to try and understand it. 'I kept asking Patrick questions, such as "what's Benediction?" But he couldn't explain things to me. Often if you are a cradle Catholic you do things naturally they are in your blood. You don't question, you just do it. You stand up at Mass, sit down, kneel down. And I was asking: why? So I decided to go on the journey of faith group at St Thomas of Canterbury in Woodford in order to find answers to these questions I had. I never really intended to be received into the Church. I just wanted answers to my questions. But gradually I moved from simply engaging with Catholicism on an intellectual level to a spiritual level.'

With her baby, Mary, on her hip, she was received into the Church at the 11.30 a.m. Mass on Pentecost Sunday 1989. She grins that this was the most nerve wracking thing she had ever done, apart from taking her driving test. 'An elderly parishioner turned to me and said, "Is that your knees knocking or is it my eyesight?"'

At this time she decided to drop out of secondary education, feeling that she wanted to teach children, not a subject. After 'dibbling and dabbling' in special needs and nursery education, Angela Myler offered her a job at St Antony's, where her children were then at school. 'Primary schools for me – and you can quote me – are the promised land.'

She heaps praise on Angela Myler for her dynamism and inspiration. 'I saw her the other night and I said to her that I had a brilliant Ofsted and it was all down to her. At the end of every year, for example, she used to write a detailed thank you letter to all her staff, not just saying thank you for being wonderful but saying thank you I was particularly pleased when you did this and I noticed you did that. What a thing to do.'

After six years at St Antony's, and having deepened her faith and knowledge of the Church through the Catholic Certificate in Religious Studies, she took up the challenge of a deputy headship at St Alban's Catholic Primary School in Havering, where she was allowed to be involved in every aspect of school life. Then in September 1999, slightly nervous but with a deep-seated belief that she was doing the right thing, she walked through the gates of St Anne's to begin to put her vision of Catholic education into place.

The role of head teacher in a Catholic school is to be a faith leader, she acknowledges, but adds that, with the changing face of education in Britain and when you are in charge of a three-quarter of a million pound budget and thirty staff, you have to wear many other hats as well. 'As a head teacher I'm also an entrepreneur, accountant, fund raiser, PR person and strategic planner.'

She says that she was delighted when her bid to the Tower Hamlets Business Partnership for a free holiday in the Isle of Wight for thirty children was successful. 'I waxed lyrical about my vision and I got it. There's a lot of money out there you can claim. And my role as a Catholic head is to try and get it. A big part of my job is raising the profile of the school. Getting the right staff is a big issue. And PR and fund raising are very important nowadays.'

Catholic schools have been called the jewel in the crown of the Church. They have come a long way since the Catholic Poor School Committee was formed in 1847, three years before the restoration of the hierarchy in England and Wales. Today there are around 740,000 children – including those of Prime Minister Tony Blair – being educated in 2,450 Catholic schools. Yet Catholic education continues to be a highly emotive topic and, occasionally, a battleground for those with differing notions of both Church and education itself.

Does Janet think, like some Catholic educationalists, that market forces pose a threat to the spiritual values that underpin Catholic education? She produces a thoughtful expression on her face. 'Yes and no. I'll go so far with that. The search for excellence is an integral part of the spiritual quest. If we are being excellent, league tables and all this data should hold no fear for us, should it? Much as we don't like them – and I don't particularly – the league tables have done a lot to make schools improve. They are forced to do it.'

So what makes a Catholic school distinctive from a state school? 'The person of Christ is so interwoven into everything we do. It's not just RE. It's everything. Some people might say, "Oh, she's being holy again." But, in fact, it's very practical. All the time you have Christ as your model. I find myself saying, what would He have done in this situation? How would He have reacted? And you only have to look in the gospels to find out. Working in an inner city school Christ's teachings about the poor have a lot of meaning. I live my faith here. I walk the walk, talk the talk and don't have to apologise for it.'

When it comes to RE, she has no doubts about what its purpose should be. 'Catholic schools are often seen as putting faith into children. This is not the purpose at all. If it happens, great. The aim of classroom RE is to make children religiously literate.' She adds that the Ofsted team had noted spiritual development in maths. 'That's what I would expect in a Catholic school. Faith development is happening but we are not doing it to the children.'

Opening a filing cabinet and taking out a copy of *The Common Good in Education*, produced by the Catholic Education Service, she points to the first page where the aims are set out. I scan my eye down them: the search for excellence, the uniqueness of the individual, education of the whole person, education of all, moral principles. She is keen on making sure that reconciliation is central to the ethos of the school. 'Our behaviour policy is based on the sacrament of reconciliation. What else could it be based on?

'People who aren't in the Catholic sector get very cross with me sometimes. They say, "Our school's got a mission statement. Our school does all those things you are describing." I say, yes it does, but my motivation is different. I'm doing this because of my beliefs.'

Feeling the need to broaden her knowledge base and acquire some new skills, she considered studying for the National Professional Qualification for Head Teachers. Instead, she became part of the first intake on the MA in Catholic School Leadership run by St Mary's College, Strawberry Hill. 'I chose this course because it addressed the same issues but from a Catholic perspective,' she says.

'In the first year of headship it's about looking as if you can do it. Credibility. The course has given me more credibility and also confidence. I've chosen practical assignments, such as mission statements, teaching and learning policy and preparing for Ofsted. I've given them to colleagues to read and they can now see where I am coming from. Part of my job now, having got here, is to train future head teachers because there is such a lack of them.'

Being a head teacher – or as she puts it self-depreciatingly 'head learner' – may be like 'riding an emotional roller coaster', but she believes she has the best job in the world. And while St Anne's presents her with some difficult challenges, she is confident that, having been given the thumbs-up from Ofsted, it and she have embarked on an exciting new era. 'I've been able to combine my own personal faith journey with my career. Journeying towards headship and journeying towards faith are inextricably linked. This is a twenty-four-hour a day job, because you wake up in the middle of the night thinking about it. It's hard to explain why it's such a good job. I suppose it's . . .' Her voice trails off and she drifts deep into thought. 'Yeah, I'm making a difference.'

The Friar

Fr Mark Elvins gives one of his boyish chuckles. 'When I was about eight I began to study chivalry and would dream of being a knight. I used to invent Arthurian names for myself – I've always been a bit eccentric, so I've been told. At my prep school and in the army I was known as King Arthur. But after I left the army I thought to myself that chivalry was dead. When I found St Francis it was like a sort of reverse mirror. Francis took hold of chivalry and turned it upside down. He took what had been a military code and turned it into a spiritual code for his community.'

I'm sitting in Fr Mark's spartan room at Greyfriars in Oxford. A coat of arms adorns a pillow on the bed; on the wall are sketches of Canterbury, Rochester and Arundel cathedrals in a single frame; and the books he's written on heraldry, liturgy, Arundel Priory and our forgotten Catholic heritage stand on a shelf next to a small statue of St Thomas Becket.

He's telling me about how he has discovered a life of romance with Christ. 'Through Francis my boyhood dreams have become a religious reality. It works for me and I think it can work for other people. They could try and see their lives as a romance with Christ. Most people see caring for the poor as a kind of drudgery; a challenge. If you have this romantic element it lifts it up and out of the gutter. On the walls of the basilica in Assisi there is an image of Francis in a mystical union in paradise with lady poverty. He took the gospel and turned it into a fine lady and wooed her. It's that essence of romanticism I find attractive.'

In his brown habit, with a bearded actor's face and an Evensong voice, Fr Mark has what you might call a classical English appearance. His Englishness is of the kind that is associated with crumbling piles, cricket on the village green and Old Testament style genealogy. He gives the impression at times of being a thirteenth-century man trapped in a twenty-first century world.

As befitting such a man, the two cities which have shaped his life the most are Oxford and Canterbury. This is his third spell in Oxford. His first was as an art student, his second as an Anglican theological student and now he is here as a Franciscan Capuchin priest. The Franciscans first took root in the city in 1224. Canterbury, where he was baptised and spent part of his childhood in The Commandant's House, has recently lured him back, to help set up a project for the city's homeless.

Gently rubbing his beard and looking up thoughtfully at the ceiling, he glows with delight at the thought of St Francis, a man who he believes has much to teach people today. 'In a sense Francis was the instrument of my conversion and a lode star in my journey of faith. The first thing I did after being received into the Church was to come here, to Greyfriars, and be received into the third order of St Francis. I was ordained on Easter Sunday 1973 at Arundel Cathedral, and it was at this point that my father had died and my mother was sick and in need of psychiatric nursing, so I had to stay in the diocese. But after she died I applied to the friars and to my amazement was accepted. And I think I'm the first priest – certainly in living memory – to have survived the novitiate.'

To enter a novitiate in your fifties is unusual. To enter a novitiate after twenty-two years as a diocesan priest is rarer still. Yet when Fr Mark looks back across his life he can see the hand of God at work. But, as is always the case, things at the time seemed far from clear.

His ability to see the humour lurking under the surface of life and, importantly, laugh at himself has, he says, served him well over the years and helped to defuse tense situations when they have arisen. Not everyone, he concedes, is able to take to his rather exuberant personality.

One of three children, he was born in Whitstable, Kent, where his mother had taken refuge from the bombs that were being dropped on Canterbury. He grew up in a rather severe-sounding middle-class family where tradition and order dictated the way life was lived. His father – who asked to be addressed as 'sir' or 'pater' – was an Anglican clergyman and the Rector of Dover Castle at the time Winston Churchill held the office of Constable there. His mother had been brought up a Catholic but abandoned her faith when she got married, although she returned to it later in life.

After his mother had a breakdown, Fr Mark found himself at the age of three in a boarding school, and by the age of six he had concluded that 'life was a raw deal'. The sugar in what seems a rather bitter childhood pill came during the time he spent with his Catholic grandparents in Farnham, Surrey, in a house he describes as resembling Thrushcroft Grange in *Wuthering Heights*.

Eventually, he was sent to Dover College, a traditional public school where cold showers and 'fagging' were as normal as Latin and Greek. It was an unhappy time of his life, he admits glumly. To escape the harsh regime, he would often sit at his desk dreaming of being a knight or a monk who spent his days illuminating manuscripts. 'I was the most beaten boy in my house. I was beaten on my first day and then regularly beaten throughout my time there by an army of prefects. Sometimes it was just for having a shoelace undone. So quite early on I got used to the down side of life. When I went home my father was so strict and Victorian that I actually preferred going back to school. At least at school you were one of a number of boys and you could melt into the crowd. At home my brother and I couldn't escape my father's punishment. I thought I'd been sold a dud hand.'

In those days sons of clergymen often entered the Church or the army. Fr Mark, somewhat reluctantly, opted for the army. 'I'd planned to study art history at the Courtauld Institute. But my father said, "I want no damn pansies in this family. You'll either join the army or get out of this house." I was kicked out of the vicarage and enlisted at the Tower of London and was accepted for a commission by the Grenadier Guards. I passed into Sandhurst but opted for a short service commission and was posted to Aldershot. I could have made a career of it but I had no intention of firing a bullet at anybody. Up to the point of commission you could leave when you wanted, so I left and took my commission in the Territorials, much more my cup of tea. You didn't have to kill people. You just played in the countryside.'

Afterwards, he went to study art at the Ruskin School, Oxford, and then joined an art dealers in St James', London. However, disenchanted by some of the practices in the art world – 'there were a lot of crooks' – and having refused to pass off a fake painting as an original to a fellow dealer, he found his dream job at Debrett's Peerage which was a 'wildly eccentric' place run by an editor who was 'splendidly dotty'. The two of them hit it off immediately and Fr Mark lodged with his new chum in his house, stuffed with ancestral portraits, on Kingston Hill. They would often go on pub crawls where they would spend the evening talking about their passion for genealogy. Fr Mark has traced his family tree back to the Norman Conquest on his mother's side and discovered the Turnhams were descendants of the castellans who manned the ramparts at Dover Castle. What's more, one of their ancestors was Ranulph de Broc who in 1170, at his Saltwood Castle home, plotted the murder of St Thomas Becket with four knights sent from France by Henry II.

Then one Sunday a friend of his father's came to preach on the feast of St Francis. 'He preached about St Francis kneeling all night and repeating "My God and my all." I went out and bought a life of St Francis and my life was turned upside down. I realised that I had been living in an ivory tower, indulging in my whimsical interest in heraldry and genealogy. I read an article in a newspaper about hopelessness. It said that hundreds of people would spend that Christmas on the streets and many would die of hypothermia.'

This led him on to the streets of the East End, where, in the evenings, he worked as a volunteer with the Anglican Brothers of Prayer and Action, based at St Botolphs-Without, Aldgate. And it was here, he says brightly, he found his vocation. 'Just as Francis was led among the lepers and only really found Christ when he embraced one, I found myself working each evening among the homeless. I saw men dying from alcoholic poisoning. I saw lives shattered by the wish for oblivion, the pain of living being too unbearable in the face of destitution. I met two young Catholic members of the Society of St Vincent de Paul. There was something about them and the way they talked about their faith.'

After three years at Debrett's he resigned and, discerning a call to ministry, returned to Oxford, this time to St Stephen's House to study theology. 'I felt my life was now beginning to make sense. I told my principal that I had read a lot about Catholicism and thought I had Roman fever. "Oh, you'll get over it," he replied, encouraging me to continue with my ordination.'

Fr Mark was ordained an Anglican at Rochester Cathedral in 1967. Despite this, his Roman fever continued throughout his first year as a curate in Gravesend. Hearing of his difficulties, his bishop instructed him to spend a month with the Community of the Resurrection, in Mirfield, Yorkshire.

'He told me that each day one of the community would shoot down my reasons for wanting to become a Catholic. Every day for a month myself and Eric Simmons, a theologian, battled for two hours over the writings of Cardinal

Newman. And then finally I discovered *The Development of Christian Doctrine*. And I thought, "That's it! I'm intellectually converted." Eric surrendered. He told me I was an absolutist and he was a relativist.'

His salary was cut off and, just as when he had abandoned a career in the army, his father greeted his decision with anger and contempt. 'I rang up the vocations director of the diocese of Westminster and said "I'm a homeless Anglican curate, destitute on the streets of London. Do you know of any good Salvation Army hostels?" He urged me to go and see Monsignor Tomlinson, a convert, at St James', Spanish Place. So I did and I was welcomed with open arms,' he giggles, throwing his head back.

For the next eighteen months he was part of a vibrant, suitably eccentric house. 'I had my first glass of whisky and saw colour TV for the first time. I spent the next eighteen months there as an honorary sacristan. It was a very entertaining place to be. The monsignor had a wide circle of rather exotic and intellectual friends, many of whom were actresses or ballerinas or involved in early music concerts.' During this time he began to feel that his life was at last making sense, and after instruction with a Jesuit at Farm Street he was received into the Catholic Church. He says now that the suffering he experienced in his childhood had a purpose. It prepared him for his future ministry as a priest.

After studies at the old St Edmund's College, Ware, Hertfordshire and the Beda College, Rome, he was ordained in Arundel Cathedral in 1973. It was while working at St Mary Magdalen, Brighton, that, in 1980, he set up the St Thomas Fund, a charity providing a residential rehabilitation programme for those who are homeless and addicted to drugs and alcohol.

He shows me a photo of a Regency street in Brighton. 'That big white house was where we started the St Thomas Fund. Christmas and Easter offerings and selling my motor car were the foundations of the first bank account.'

He bought the house freehold through anonymous

donations worth £44,000, which he found after returning from a pilgrimage to Canterbury, where he had prayed at the site of St Thomas Becket's martyrdom. 'Whenever we needed money I'd go on pilgrimage to Canterbury and something would always turn up. So St Thomas was nicknamed "old golden bones".'

Fr Mark claims enthusiastically that 80% of those who have been through programmes run by the St Thomas Fund at their three houses leave drug and alcohol free. This sounds astonishing, I suggest, But how does he know? 'We stay in touch with people. The figure of 80% is related to those we are in touch with. Many are on courses or in employment.

'We are reversing hopelessness. Most charities contain homelessness. They don't necessarily reverse it. We need night shelters, we need soup runs, we need hostels. But the causes of hopelessness need to be addressed as well. You have to treat individuals as of value. If you treat them as important it enables them to gain their self-respect, which eventually orchestrates their own recovery. Homelessness covers those who are destitute on the street to those who have no fixed or protected tenancy. Anyone can be made homeless through a tragedy or a sudden weakness for alcohol and drugs.' He goes on to tell me about doctors, university teachers, army officers and even priests who have presented themselves as homeless at the St Thomas Fund.

Homelessness is an opportunity for evangelisation, he suggests, not through preaching but through reflecting the love and compassion of Jesus and through living with the poor. 'If you can help homeless people to accept themselves you can win.' He points out that St Thomas used to invite the poor into his palace at Canterbury and wash their feet.

Since becoming a Capuchin – he's now the vocations director – Fr Mark has confined his involvement with the St Thomas Fund to the role of spiritual director. He is, however, hoping to repeat the success of the St Thomas

Fund in Canterbury, where a similar programme, Beckett Homes, was launched in 2000.

So what was it like entering the Capuchin novitiate as a priest in 1995? 'I just knuckled down and bit my lip,' he replies with a banana smile. 'I suddenly found myself in my fifties cleaning lavatories and picking up leaves. Although the friars were kind and gentle, psychologically I had to bite my lip and keep my head down. I had all these youngsters telling me what to do. I was so determined to get through. As an Anglican in 1965 I dreamed I died in a Capuchin habit. I think the Capuchins thought, "This man is a sticker, so we'll give him a chance." I'm naturally exceedingly stubborn. I tell people in advance,' he says candidly, then breaking into raucous laughter, 'I'm like a terrier with a slipper.'

When I ask him about the kind of spirituality he has, he points to the crucifix above his bed and says keenly, 'That cross for some people is a threat. But for those who believe it is a sign of love and triumph; the triumph of love. By submission and suffering Jesus conquered the world. God as God is beyond our comprehension. God as Man is the bridge between Heaven and earth.'

It has been said that religion is simply organised spirituality. But spirituality must touch the heart as well as the head, insists Fr Mark. 'I've had the good fortune to take two degrees in spirituality, at Heythrop in London and the Milltown Institute in Dublin. Now, I only say this because theology by itself can be simply an intellectual exercise. It has to be linked to spirituality because spirituality is theology lived. The one thing lacking in my seminary training was spirituality. When I hear in the university hall where I live people discussing Thomist philosophy and the scholastic approach, I feel it needs a more spiritual application. Studying spirituality has given me a whole new perspective and enabled me to translate my faith into experience and then share it with others.'

He returns to his recurring ideas about chivalry, romance and kingship which are never far from the surface. 'When Christ prepared to enter Jerusalem he consciously went to Bethphage and mounted an ass and then rode into Jerusalem. The route from Bethphage to Jerusalem was the coronation route used by King Solomon. In Israel kings who set out to make war travelled on horseback. When they came to make peace they travelled on asses. Hence Our Lord's procession on an ass. And Jesus entered the city by the Beautiful Gate, which the Ottomans blocked up when they conquered Jerusalem. There is a saying that the Beautiful Gate will not be unstopped until Christ returns in glory. He was vested in mocking purple and given reeds as a mocking sceptre and crowned with thorns. And, as with all kings, he was presented to the people, by Pontius Pilate. Eventually he was enthroned upon the cross. Now I very much see the idea of kingship not in a political way but in the context of sacral of suffering kingship. Jesus is a king who dies for his people and he rules not by force but by the bonds of love. I think that when we come before Christ we will not receive a judgement meted out by Christ but one that is self-inflicted. We will willingly go to purgatory because we will feel so unworthy of such love. One thing the Puritans got right under Cromwell was when they said "there is no king but Jesus" because he rules our hearts and lives.

'Many knights used to pledge themselves to Our Lady. St Richard of Chichester, when he was a student, here in Oxford, took off his gold ring and put it on the finger of the statue of Our Lady in the university church and pledged his celibacy to her. So when I became a Catholic I went to Walsingham and took off my gold signet ring and gave it to the shrine as a pledge of my celibacy. I like the romantic gesture. It gives colour to a vocation and turns my life into a kind of stained glass window.'

So how does he envisage eternity? 'I think it's beyond our comprehension,' he answers with a look of wonderment. 'St Paul says somewhere that the mind cannot conceive what God has in store for those who love Him. The closest we get, I think, is in Luke's gospel. Martha was busying herself in the kitchen and getting no help from Mary, who is kneeling at Our Lord's feet and adoring him. Jesus said to her, "Martha, Martha you are busy about many things but only one thing is important, to love God; Mary has chosen the better part." In the end it is the contemplative life which is the greatest, not in any pejorative sense. But this is our destiny; to sit at the feet of God and adore. But we can't understand this in our finite condition on earth. But when we have risen and are reunited with our glorified body and soul we will have a new knowledge and understanding. Images, art, poetry and the examples of the saints are the only way we can try to understand this.'

There is, he is convinced, a new, or second, spring of Catholicism in Oxford, spearheaded by very bright converts, such as John Saward and Stratford Caldecott. 'They often have a wisdom and an understanding of Catholicism that, perhaps, cradle Catholics don't have. A deep and profound hold permeates their whole lives. And what is interesting at somewhere like the Oratory is what packs them in: traditional liturgy, orthodox belief and a kind of permeation of their faith throughout their whole life.'

Fr Mark is also the author of *Catholic Trivia*, a fascinating book which reveals, amongst other things, that the roots of carnival are in the Latin words *carnis*, 'flesh', and *levare*, 'to remove', and the name signified the abstinence from flesh meats after Shrove Tuesday. And until the Reformation thirteen was considered a lucky number. What's more, 'dunce' derives from the name of the mediaeval theologian Duns Scotus and was a derogatory term for his followers. And 'hocus pocus' is a parody of the words of consecration in the Mass, *Hoc est corpus*.

So what led him to research the book? 'It had been in my head since I was a schoolboy. I used to get bored watching cricket, so I'd invent historical quizzes. I wrote it while I was in bed during my convalescence after an accident in 1990,' he replies casually.

Driving me through the centre of Oxford back to the station, he tells me Oxford has more priests per square mile than any other city in Britain. He then provides a running commentary on the Catholic roots of many of the colleges we pass. 'That's Worcester. It was Gloucester Hall for the monks of Gloucester Abbey. Wadham was an Augustinian house. The Cistercians founded St John's. They were nearly all begun by religious orders.' There is a wistful note in his voice. He is, I suspect, thinking of that second spring.

The Tycoon

I had been fascinated, and tickled, by a rather bizarre story in the *Catholic Times* in April 1999 headlined 'Telegraph owner in "bishop is a twerp" row.' According to the report, Conrad Black had accused Bishop Frederick Henry of Calgary in Canada of being 'a jumped-up little twerp' and 'a useful idiot'.

So what triggered Mr Black to indulge in a spot of bishop bashing? It appears that there had been a five-month strike at the *Calgary Herald*, which is owned by Mr Black. Bishop Henry, in an article in the *Western Catholic Reporter*, had, apparently, defended the workers. The bishop, sticking to good solid Catholic social teaching, said the workers had a right to strike and then took a swipe at Mr Black for, says the *Catholic Times*, 'insulting his workers, failing to consider their legitimate demands and adopting an intransigent approach to the dispute.' Mr Black responded via the *National Post*, castigating the bishop for 'running off at the episcopal mouth' and wading into the *Herald*'s dispute without hearing the side of the management. Stung by this, the bishop said, 'I regard the comments as cheap shots. I think they are hitting below the belt.'

Nevertheless, the bishop, true to his calling, added that he forgave Mr Black. 'I think that basically my response to him has got to be a Christ-like response, and that's basically to forgive him. In the heat of the moment he probably got carried away and said something that I'm sure he now regrets.' The heads of Calgary's churches stood shoulder to shoulder with Bishop Henry, labelling Mr Black's remarks as 'outrageous' and 'unchristian'. In an impressive display of ecumenical solidarity, they added, 'The Church of Calgary is united. When outsiders choose to attack one of us, they attack us all.'

Several conclusions can be drawn from this episode: Mr Black is no respecter of episcopal status when he feels he is in the right, one should tread carefully in any kind of dispute, and don't mess with Church leaders in Calgary. I don't know who was right and who was wrong in this unedifying yet highly entertaining little spat, but, I suspect, Mr Black hasn't risen to the dizzy heights of Canary Wharf by being meek and mild. The dispute has since been resolved, along the lines the management proposed. When I sent the draft chapter to Mr Black for approval he wrote back: 'There is no collective agreement, no union recognition, no closed shop and none of the other scleroses that the bishop in his innocence had been cajoled into espousing.'

All I knew about Conrad Black was that, like Rupert Murdoch and the late Robert Maxwell, he is what is often termed a 'newspaper baron'. He is clearly very wealthy and powerful, the man behind the *Telegraph* group of newspapers and also, interestingly, on the board of the *Catholic Herald*. 'He's a convert, you know,' claimed a priest friend of mine as we chatted about the story one afternoon in The Cardinal pub behind Westminster Cathedral. 'Really!' I replied. 'Yes. Why not try and get him for the book?'

Having always operated on the journalistic principle that potential interviewees can only say no, or, as sometimes happens with well known names, not reply at all, I sat down at my Apple Mac and wrote what I thought was a rather optimistic letter to Mr Black at his *Telegraph* office at Canary Wharf.

A few days later, to my surprise, I received an e-mail from one of his assistants, explaining that Mr Black had dealt with his conversion in a chapter of his autobiography, which I was welcome to see. But could I send some information about the publisher, the book, and myself? So – I e-mailed back that the book was to be published by Gracewing, a small Catholic company, and that it was an attempt to chart the faith journeys of an eclectic group of Catholics. I said that I was a journalist, thirty-nine years of age, lived in south-east London, and had remained a Catholic, despite a few falls from grace along the road of faith. To add the human touch, I explained that I had a three-year-old daughter, but was separated from my wife.

Nothing happened for a couple of weeks and then one morning a letter arrived from Rosemary Millar, Mr Black's PA, with a photocopy of the relevant chapter of Mr Black's autobiography. I sent another e-mail, expressing my thanks but asking if Mr Black could answer the following questions:

How does his faith influence his business practice?

How should the Church in the West respond to an increasingly secular society and mind set?

What has been his strongest experience of God in his life?

Which modern Catholic writers inspire him?

What is his view on the pontificate of Pope John Paul II?

I could have thought of lots more questions, but I didn't want to overdo it, and I felt these five would act as a door for him to reveal something of his own faith and attitudes, if he so wished.

Soon after, a reply came back from Ms Millar:

> Dear Mr Watts,
> Thank you for your letter of 19 May which I have shown to Mr Black.
>
> He says that you are welcome to use the piece from his book which he sent to you and I also enclose some biographical details for your information.

> He declines to respond to your first three questions but the answer to the fourth is Cardinal Newman. If you don't think he's sufficiently modern, then he nominates G. K. Chesterton, Charles de Gaulle and William Buckley.
>
> His opinion of the pontificate of Pope John Paul II is 'an inspiring success, only slightly diminished by his monastic view on sexual matters, which I take as a counsel of perfection, like the Sermon on the Mount.'

Although I hadn't succeeded in enticing the lion out of his cage, Mr Black's choice of writers was interesting: two of the greatest Catholic minds since the Reformation, completely orthodox in their theology and both converts. On the other hand, I knew little about the writings of Charles de Gaulle and I had never – to my shame – heard of William Buckley. A quick flick through my Catholic encyclopaedia revealed that William Buckley was born in 1925 and is 'a conservative Catholic opinion leader in the United States', being one of the founders of the American conservative movement. He also established, in 1955, the *National Review*, described as 'America's leading conservative journal of opinion'.

Mr Black's biographical information presents a picture of a extremely bright, shrewd, ambitious, wealthy and complex man. Born in Canada in 1944, he gained a first degree at Carleton University and then followed it up with further degrees at McGill University and Laval University. He is chairman and chief executive of the multinational company Hollinger International Inc., which controls or has interests in over 400 publications including the *Daily Telegraph*, *The Spectator*, the *Jerusalem Post*, the *Montreal Gazette* and the *Chicago Sun-Times*. In addition, he is a director of a number of other companies and a member of bodies such as the International Institute for Strategic Studies and the Institute for International Economics.

He is married to newspaper and magazine columnist Barbara Amiel, who is also editorial vice-president of

Hollinger International. He has two sons and a daughter by his previous marriage.

So what of his journey to Catholicism? It is clear from reading the chapter from his autobiography that Mr Black has clearly read both deeply and widely and at one time, he reveals, even toyed with the idea of becoming a psychoanalyst until he saw that theology rather than psychology offered the key to understanding human existence. Amongst others, Freud, Darwin, Copernicus, Gibbon, Russel and Napoleon are brought into his discussion about the existence of God. 'I have never been able to state, as Newman did, that I was sure of God's existence "as of the existence of my own hands and feet"' remarks Mr Black at one point. Later, he states that he accepts Newman's view 'that our conscience, "powerful, peremptory, unargumentative, irrational, minatory and definitive", is God speaking in our minds.' All of this gives you a picture of a man sitting up in his armchair late into the night, books laid out at his feet, wrestling with that question Pilate put to Jesus: what is truth?

It wasn't until 1986 that Mr Black 'formally converted' to Catholicism and began going to Mass. He was received with his elder son in the private chapel of Cardinal Emmet Carter, the Archbishop of Toronto. He goes on to describe how and why he made the decision:

> I eventually reasoned that from belief in the existence of a deity it was a comparatively easy step to believe that the Deity had heavily influenced Christ (though not Christ alone) and that Christ invited St Peter to found a church and that the Roman Catholic Church, 'for all its inanities, vulgarities and compromises', as Cardinal Leger once put it to me, is the legitimate continuator of the early Christians.
>
> Logically, once launched on this course, it was not possible for me to avoid the conclusion that if I wished to communicate with the creator of the universe, the surest means, though neither a sure means nor the only

means of doing so, was to receive the sacraments from the Roman Catholic priesthood. Once intellect and intuition united to convince me that the spiritual life was real and useful, I was resistless against the benign temptations of religious practice, though my adherence was delayed for seven years waiting for the annulment of my first wife's marriage and has been well short of zealous since.

I had read the relevant thoughts of many other prominent converts beside Newman, including Edith Sitwell and Evelyn Waugh, and especially Chesterton and his desire 'to be rid of my sins' and discussed it with Muggeridge, I did have some sympathy for Rebecca West, who gave up her Catholic preparations when she tired of being sermonised to by homosexual priests. I even found Marshall McLuhan's comments on the same subject, unlike most of his reflections, rather profound.

Fortunately, my Catholic religious instruction consisted of countless pleasant evenings over fine claret in the home of Cardinal Emmet Carter, reciting Newman and others to each other. 'I looked in the mirror and saw a monophysite', said Newman, so the Cardinal reminded me in one of his Christmas cards. I eventually concluded that I believed in the occasional occurrence of miracles and that if a miracle can happen, logically any miracle can, even the virgin birth and the physical ascension of Christ. But I couldn't go further than to acknowledge that they and other such scientifically improbable events might have happened.

The Cardinal assured me that I was still eligible, as long as I accepted the resurrection, 'without which', His Eminence unequivocally averred, of his entire personal faith and professional life, 'it is all a fraud and trumpery'. Dear and deeply respected friend though Cardinal Carter already was, I could not fail to admire him even more as a highly learned and talented person who had frankly gambled his entire life on an intelligent and precise act of faith.

As you might expect from someone with such a rigorous and inquiring mind, he had explored Protestantism in its various forms, but concluded that it was just 'a congregationalist gesture by those who found agnosticism imprudent or unsustainable.' He also sees it as a nationalistic rather than a universal faith.

Despite his admiration for Newman and Chesterton, he parts company with them on sexual matters, preferring to take a live and let live line. 'I continue to be entirely tolerant of the full range of beliefs and disbeliefs, of intense religious observance and complete abstention. With religion, as with sex, people should do what they want, avoid what they don't want, be discreet, and respect the views of others.'

Looking back over his life, he says that he had never been happy with his confirmation as an Anglican while a student at Upper Canada College, and had concluded that his father's 'nihilistic atheism' was 'barren, unremitting and illogical. Of course spiritual forces exist; of course there is a God by some definition, before whom humility is appropriate, if not required. The world is not just an accident and life is sacred in general and valuable, though not inviolable, in all cases. "Can he be less than divine?" asked Napoleon of Christ. I think not, and by 1986 I had lived in evasive apostasy long enough.'

After firing a broadside at 'trendy clerics mouthing socialist platitudes and depicting God as our pal jogging along beside us' – reminiscent of his attack on Bishop Henry – he concludes this chapter with his assessment of the Catholic Church. 'I do commend Catholicism to those so inclined. It is not a panacea, but it's sane, rigorous and consoling and the human spirit and intelligence can be comfortable with it.

'My father used to cite the French philosophical aphorism that life leads "to suicide or the foot of the cross". I believe the choice need not be so stark, but he and others of my acquaintance who avoided any serious intellectual effort to reconcile themselves to the unkind limitations imposed in the nature of life paid a heavy price in mental strife.'

The Marxist Historian

Professor David McLellan is one of the world's leading experts on Marxism. His students might, perhaps, expect him to share Marx's view that religion is 'the opium of the people'. Far from it. Professor McLellan is a committed Catholic, who once walked 450 miles on pilgrimage through Spain.

I arrive at his quaint seventeenth-century house in the centre of Canterbury, where in the seventh century St Augustine founded an abbey and began bringing the Christian message to the Anglo-Saxon tribes. Nearly six hundred years later, with the country then Christian, St Thomas Becket, the Archbishop of Canterbury, was murdered in the city's cathedral when he opposed attempts by Henry II to usurp the power of the Church.

With these thoughts running through my mind I wait for David. No reply. I push the bell again, taking his letter out of my jacket pocket and wondering if I have the right day.

Just then I hear a voice and turn around to see a smiling, tall slim man, clutching a Safeway carrier bag. With his wisps of white hair retreating from the crown of his head, and slightly startled face behind thin glasses, he looks far less severe than I had imagined a professor of political theory and author of numerous books, some of which have been translated into thirteen languages, to be.

'You were beginning to wonder if you'd got the right

day, weren't you?' he greets me cheerily, as he turns the key and leads me into the house, explaining that he has just come from the Citizen's Advice Bureau, where he works as a regular volunteer adviser.

We emerge into a room stuffed with books from the floor to the low ceiling. Under a mountain range of papers, notes, airmail envelopes, pens and journals, a desk can just about be discerned. I later learn that so impressed were Channel 4 by the clutter on his desk that they filmed him through the window, sitting there when he was presenting a programme he had written about the radical French thinker, social activist and spiritual writer Simone Weil. The walls are decorated with photos, paintings, sketches, postcards and newspaper cuttings.

He motions me into another room towards a table, and suggests we begin the interview while he puts on some soup. I nod absentmindedly, glancing around at more books, journals scattered here and there, a copy of *Le Monde* on a chair, an aerial photo of Canterbury, a large, fraying sketch of Karl Marx, knick-knacks from around the world, including carved wooden figures around a crib, and photos of his family. Over the door to his kitchen is pinned the motto 'For evil to triumph, it is only necessary that good men do nothing'.

So when and why did he become a Catholic? I begin. 'I converted in 1959 – or was it 1958? – when I was at Oxford,' he replies from the kitchen. 'A good friend of mine was largely responsible for it I suppose,' he says in a mellow, unhurried voice as he returns to the room and sits down opposite me.

That friend who, he says, 'presented me with the possibility of becoming a Catholic', was Cormac Rigby, who went on to become one of the best known voices on BBC Radio 3 – before confounding his colleagues at Broadcasting House by turning his back on his career in broadcasting to train for the priesthood.

David adds that, as you might expect, his conversion was fairly intellectual. He had investigated various Christian traditions before arriving at the conclusion that it was only the Catholic Church that could trace its roots back through the centuries to the New Testament.

'I thought to myself that all these Christian churches have got a bit of the truth, while the Catholic Church had a more rounded truth. It was, on the surface, a rational process. Reading Catholic apologetics I was impressed by how they explained doctrines,' he says, attempting to summarise what, I suspect, was a more complicated process.

He began accompanying his friend to 7.15 a.m. Mass each day at St Aloysius church and, like many fresh to Catholicism, found the ritual and symbolism fascinating. Eventually he received instruction from a Dominican priest and was baptised.

Fired with zeal after his conversion, he felt drawn towards life as a Jesuit, the most intellectually rigorous religious order in the Catholic Church. But six months in the spartan Jesuit novitiate in Grantham, Lincolnshire, taught him that his vocation lay elsewhere.

In 1960 he went to live in Paris, where he taught at the Jesuit School of Ste Genevieve and attended lectures at the Sorbonne. It was here that he was inspired by Ad Lucem, a radical Catholic group committed to social justice and to making the gospel relevant to the lives of ordinary people.

Even now, he talks about this interlude in his life with great enthusiasm. It was indeed one of those pivotal moments in life and for David it resulted in him choosing to specialise in Marxism. 'I saw that French Catholics had integrated their faith with politics. And I thought this was marvellous. Ad Lucem was very much concerned with global technical co-operation and the meeting of cultures. The still rather ghettoised Catholicism I had joined in England made very little connection between religious belief and social and political involvement. In Ad Lucem I met people whose Catholic faith and progressive commitment were all of a piece. This made a profound impression which, fortunately, has never deserted me.'

He became a Catholic at the time when the Church was entering a major period of renewal under the Second Vatican Council, which met between 1962–65. Around 2,600 Catholic bishops from all over the world convened to debate and discuss how the Church was to respond to the challenges of the modern world.

'Vatican II was grist to my mill. I thought it was progressive,' he enthuses, putting a bowl of thick, steaming soup in front of me along with a plate of falafel. 'I'm vegetarian,' he explains, half apologetically.

Born in 1940, one of three children, he grew up in Hertford in what he describes as a 'straightforward, calm, middle-class family.' Although his father taught Greek and Latin at University College, London, he says his family were not well off. Unlike his father, his mother was a Christian, and she took him to a Congregational chapel.

'The reading and preaching of the Bible was very strong,' he recalls, adding after a pause, 'it made a deep impression on me.' Catholics, however, were to be avoided. 'When I was growing up a lot of people had said Rome was the whore of Babylon.' He laughs.

Marx's ideas of dialectical materialism and the dictatorship of the proletariat may not be as fashionable as they once were when they brought down governments in some countries and shaped social policy in others. But David believes that even though Marx developed an atheistic ideology there is much to learn from it about the workings of society. 'Marxism provides the best analysis of society but is weak on saying what should be done about it. Marx has a profound account of the reasons for oppression and inequality in our society. This is of obvious concern to Christians interested in social justice. His ideas have not, though, shaped Catholic theology much, given the huge, and only recently slightly modified, antipathy between the two. Of course, they both share an opposition to the individualistic, market-orientated *zeitgeist*. The influence is most marked in liberation theology which, particularly in the 1960s and 1970s, took over a lot of Marx's social theory to provide an empirical underpinning for Catholic social thought. This provided a strong stimulus for the emancipatory thrust which is integral to the Christian message.'

Telescoping back to the late sixties and early seventies, when he was teaching in both Britain and the US, he says that Marxism went beyond purely academic interest. 'Sometimes the atmosphere recalled that of the fourth-century Arian heresy which revolved around the question of whether Jesus was of like substance to the Father or of one substance – homoousios or homoiousios – the difference of two letters – but which threatened the foundations of the Roman Empire.'

Having established himself as a leading figure in the world of Marxist thought, in 1974 he was made Professor of Political Theory at the University of Kent at Canterbury. However, this coincided with the break-up of his marriage and his wife returning to live in France with their two daughters. He sees both his daughters, and his grandchildren, regularly. One daughter lives in Paris, the other, by a quirk of fate, he suggests, in Canterbury.

So does his Catholicism seep into his tutorials and seminars? He replies that he encourages his students to think creatively and critically, which is, after all, what the Church does. 'As an academic you're committed to intellectual honesty and truth-seeking.'

In 1990, at the age of fifty, he packed his rucksack, slipped in St Augustine's *Confessions* and Simone Weil's *Notebooks*, and undertook a pilgrimage to the shrine of St James the Apostle in Santiago de Compostela, Spain. Modestly, he says that he only walked 450 of the 800 miles. That must have worked out at around fifteen miles a day, I suggest. He nods and then adds that it probably wasn't a wise thing to do at such an age.

'A friend of mine, Alan Ecclestone, who was a Communist Party member as well as an Anglican clergyman, talked to me a lot about his walks in the south of France. I was coming up to fifty and wanted to think about the second half/third of my life. It was a wonderful experience. I remember the sheer pleasure of walking in beautiful, open and uninhabited countryside. I had a couple of experiences bordering on the mystical. I found myself crying uncontrollably at the Port della Gloria at the entrance to the Cathedral at Saintpaco. Like all pilgrims, I, of course, received my scallop shell. Needless to say, I drank a fair quantity of really cold and dry white wine.'

Today, he teaches political theory at Goldsmith's College, University of London, while still keeping his hand in at Canterbury where he supervises a few Ph.D. students. So, who would he say has been the major influence on his life as a Christian? Simone Weil, he says without hesitating.

Born into a distinguished Jewish family in Paris, Simone Weil, a contemporary of Jean Paul Sartre, was seized by Marx's ideas and served with the International Brigade against Franco in the Spanish Civil War. Returning to France, she worked as a labourer on farms and in factories, moving nearer and nearer to Christianity in her thought but never feeling able to be baptised. She died in Ashford, Kent, in 1943, having had several mystical experiences.

'Most people espouse a set of principles that don't fully connect with the way they live. There's a gap. When I was making the Channel 4 film and asked people who knew her what was the most striking thing about her, they said that there was no gap between her values and her practice. There was an honesty about the way she conducted herself. She had a brilliant mind and was strikingly original. Her message today is that of the patron saint of outsiders. She shows you can have a passionate devotion to the Catholic faith and not exclude other religious traditions. She also shows how you can combine a solidarity with the poor and an uncompromising attachment to absolute spiritual values.'

How has his image of God changed since his conversion? 'At the time of my conversion I was thinking about God in quite a specific way. I tried to pin him down. I now think in a more fluid way. I now think about what God isn't rather than what God is. Simone Weil said it doesn't depend on us whether or not we believe in God, but it does depend on us not to depend on false Gods.'

He draws spiritual strength and insight from the stories contained in the Bible, which is better understood as a library spanning 1000 years of writing than as a single book. 'Reading the Gospels still makes a huge impression on me. I see the Gospels as messages. But the meaning of a biblical text is not self-evident. If we ask what did Plato, Hobbes or Marx mean we have to recreate their world. Things always need interpretation.'

Since the late 1980s he has been a member of the Bishops' Conference of England and Wales Committee for the World of Work, which discusses topical issues concerning employment, such as the European Union directives on the minimum wage and the 48-hour week, and then pressures the government to introduce or modify legislation in the light of the principles of Catholic views on social justice.

During the day, he will put his books and notes to one side, sit in silence and reflect on his life. 'When I go to church I light a candle, kneel down and pray. People who say, "I can be a Christian without going to church . . ."' His voice trails off as she shakes his head in a gently disapproving I-don't-know kind of way.

Looking back over the years does he, like some, see the hand of God at work in his life? 'I don't see a pattern in my life of God leading me. But I do see God presenting me with one challenge or new phase after another.'

And doubts? 'No more than I have doubts about being British. But I do often about its meaning and my responses.' But how does he reconcile the suffering in, say, Auschwitz or famine-stricken Ethiopia in the 1980s with an all powerful, loving creator? 'Maybe God also suffers, as a mother does when her child is ill. And holocausts and famines are the responsibilities of humans too.'

So, then, Heaven, how does he imagine it? He thinks for

a moment and then tentatively responds that 'conviviality' would sum it up, perhaps. 'Yes, conviviality. A lot of images in the Gospels are of houses and feasts. In my Father's house there are many mansions.'

The Artist

What would you do if someone told you that they had gone Christmas shopping with Christ in Oxford Street? My guess is you would make 'mm' sounds and then try to politely extricate yourself from the conversation as quickly as possible. Well, I didn't do that. For two hours I sat at the kitchen table of Elizabeth Wang's Harpenden home and listened with fascination as she explained her amazing and extraordinary relationship with Christ. And I came away thinking not that she was a bit short of a shilling – as, I have to confess, I had thought I might – but deeply impressed by the ring of truth to her words and, yes, a little astonished.

Harpenden in Hertfordshire is not the first place you would expect to encounter someone who claims to have, what are technically called, private revelations. An Italian village or a medieval convent, maybe. But Harpenden? With its wide High Street of estate agents, restaurants, garden furniture shops, Sainsburys and the profusion of people-carriers ferrying children to ballet and piano classes, it has that genteel, slightly lazy and prosperous feel of so many Home Counties dormitory towns. This is what the political commentators like to label as 'Middle England'. Medjugorje or San Giovanni Rotondo it is not.

Elizabeth lives in a red-brick detached house, just off the High Street and in the same road as the quaint Our Lady of Lourdes Catholic church, where her son Stephen was ordained by Cardinal Hume in 1998. In fact, it's Stephen who opens the door to me. He leads me towards the kitchen and tells me that he's spent the night at home but is shortly returning to his north London parish.

My first impression of Elizabeth is of someone who would pass for an agony aunt. A cross between Clare Rayner and Ann Atkins. Wearing a long blue blouse, beige skirt, slightly plump, with a warm, motherly face behind thin spectacles, and her greying hair tied in a bun, she is clutching a walking stick. In 1989, after years of a mystery illness, she was diagnosed with a mild form of multiple sclerosis. In her soothing voice that carries within it traces of a Mancunian accent, she sits down at the table and tells me she has made some sandwiches in case I get hungry.

The kitchen is clearly the nerve centre of the home. A bookcase stands near the window through which is a garden long enough to stage the FA Cup Final. A pile of newspapers are stacked on a chair, a bottle of tomato ketchup on a shelf, while on the walls are an icon of Christ, post-its, and a huge painting of Harpenden Common in summer. A vase of yellow carnations and lilies and the cards hanging up are, I later discover, the remainders of a party the previous weekend to mark her husband Kin's retirement as an eye surgeon from the NHS. On the table next to various papers and odds and ends is a poster of some of her Mass paintings. Using swirls of light, these are quite stunning images of the hidden and spiritual significance of the Mass.

These paintings, she says without any hint of embarrassment or self-importance, are part of a mission given to her by Christ. The other parts of this mission are her books which, she claims, contain messages, or teachings, from Christ on prayer and the spiritual life, and Radiant Light, a new movement she has set up to renew the faith of Catholics and others seeking Christ. 'I've never painted fantasy. And these other paintings follow on because they are only what came before me when I was praying. Not with my bodily eyes. These are the things that Our Lord showed me.'

When I ask her to describe her style of painting she says that she's always been a realist, even from her childhood. 'I was a botanical painter, exhibiting in London for years. But this changed. I found that I couldn't do the detailed work anymore because of multiple sclerosis. I became a bit clumsy. But I wanted to carry on painting. I decided to use a big brush and large canvasses and try to paint a prayer, a subject that had always fascinated me, but I didn't know how to do it. So I painted a couple of pictures showing impressions of the light of prayer and the interior of a church. Catholics wouldn't find Mass boring or dull if they really understood the staggering significance of it and how it unites earth with Heaven,' she adds brightly.

It was in December 1985 that Elizabeth's remarkable experience of Christ in Oxford Street took place and consequently led to the 'spiritual marriage' which transformed her life. In fact, the acute presence of Christ began that morning as she sat on the train to St Pancras.

'I couldn't see him but he felt more real than anything. Conversation in the spiritual life can be about words but they are not said out loud. But when you are very close to Christ, or to a saint, in a spiritual experience or spiritual bond, one can communicate a feeling which doesn't need words. Yet it's not a wishy-washy, nice-to-be-together feeling. It's a way of communication of mind to mind without words. And it's wonderful because there is never any shadow of misunderstanding. I couldn't go in any shops because I was conversing with him and was overwhelmed with the joy he was giving me. This came at the end of very difficult times. I had experienced many years of darkness in prayer, which he had allowed me to go through. This was the moment when he showed me all the testing was over. I was coming out of the dark night.'

Since then, she claims to have seen Christ on hundreds of occasions and the Virgin Mary on others. Understandably, some people will find all of this incredible and dismiss Elizabeth as at best deluded or, at worst, a charlatan. Yes, they might conclude charitably, her heart and faith may be in the right place, but to claim that Christ was with her on a shopping trip is, well, preposterous. The day before, in conversation with a priest, I mentioned I was going to interview a woman who received private revelations. He just pulled a face and swiftly skated over the subject.

Elizabeth knows what some people might think of her story and she is well aware of the cautious approach needed when addressing private revelations. Since they began, she has met with her local bishop and has submitted all her writings for examination to a Jesuit, who has concluded that they contain orthodox Catholic teachings, as well as to her previous and current parish priest. Most of her books have received the imprimatur; others are waiting for official approval. 'There's been no official statement but I'm allowed to put out books in the church and notices on the board,' she says matter-of-factly.

For eight years, she only told her family and close friends about these words of knowledge from God. 'I didn't think it right to go around telling people my life story at the drop of a hat; nor did I think it right to tell people about wonderful prayer experiences. Then Christ asked me to write down his words. This horrified me. He also asked me to go and see my parish priest at the time, Fr O'Leary. If you like, the gloves were off. Christ has told me what to do next for the last ten years, so I've literally followed his instructions. He asked me to get involved in catechesis, which isn't what I would have chosen because I didn't think I was qualified. The local priest took me on and I got involved and wrote things about the Eucharist. The Lord had taught me how to teach the Eucharist and then he asked me to put that in a book, which I did. It's called *How to Pray*.

'In Church terms, I've led a sheltered life. I've always worshipped locally. And because I have been busy with my three children and my work I haven't had the leisure to go to conferences or running after visionaries or whatever until recently. I've tried to read widely, but have stuck mainly to the classical spiritual writers, such as Jean-Pierre de Caussade and the Abbot Joseph Marmion, the Scriptures and the teachings of the Church.'

One of her books is called *Falling in Love: A Spiritual Autobiography*. It runs to 732 pages and is copiously indexed. How would she summarise the messages of Christ? Are there messages specific to the present day, for example? Or is it simply a restatement of the Gospel? 'It's both but there are several aspects to it,' she replies. 'It's first of all a joyful message because he's saying through these pictures, teachings and talks, "I'm still alive. Everything the Church teaches about me is true. And I can change your lives and make you happy." That's the main plank, but there's another aspect to it. There's so much concern with specialisation and qualification. Ordinary Catholics are frightened to speak about Church teaching because there are so many experts around and some of them say it's not like that or it's changed. Our Lord is saying the heart of Catholic teaching has not changed. Don't put any labels on me. I'm not a traditionalist, or left, or right. I'm just an ordinary Catholic. What really counts is that we try to love God and our neighbour and be obedient to the Church. It's very simple.' She adds warmly that it doesn't matter if you feel you have made a mess of your life. 'The important thing is to keep returning to Christ.'

So, then, how does she imagine Heaven? I suggest that we are used to doing things which have a beginning and an end, a sunset, a cup of coffee, a conversation, for example. How do we connect experiences such as these with life everlasting?

'I think you've put it all together because the sunset, the cup of coffee and the conversation are all about beauty, refreshment and community. I know this sounds a bit heavy, but Heaven is not something I imagine; it's something I know. It's a meeting with God the Holy Trinity, who is the most glorious, loving, perfect and fulfilling end we could arrive at. Even now we live in the Communion of Saints. We're all spiritually united. So, in Heaven, we'll all be together in a way which, as St Paul says, will surpass our wildest dreams. There will be no barriers between us, no prejudices, bad habits or suspicion keeping us apart, no pain.'

So would we do things in Heaven? Walking, for example? 'If we are going to be strictly accurate about the spiritual life we have to say there will be no material things such as paint brushes and refrigerators. The essence of Heaven is the worship and adoration of God. This is the most blissful experience you could have. Everything blissful we experience on earth is borrowed from bliss in God. It's a foretaste of Heaven.'

One of three children, Elizabeth grew up as an Anglican. Both her parents were teachers. The early part of her childhood was spent in Slough, Berkshire, and then when her father returned home after the Second World War they moved to a village outside Amersham in Buckinghamshire.

From the age of thirteen, she says, she began to question why there were so many churches. 'I was taught the branch theory but I didn't believe it. God seemed like a headmaster or a policeman. I stopped going to church. This was a deliberate decision, not to join in something I didn't understand and in a church I didn't understand. I was always fascinated by God. But I couldn't work out who he was or what he was like. And I didn't know which Church was telling the truth about him.' Reading a paperback about the life of the Spanish mystic St Teresa of Avila had intrigued her, but it didn't lead her to the Catholic Church, though it may have sown seeds.

She had always painted ever since she was little and bought her paint boxes at jumble sales. But it was a career in nursing, not art, that she chose after leaving school. While working at University College Hospital, London, she met and fell in love with a young trainee eye-doctor, the son of Chinese immigrants who had settled in

Sheffield. The Mills and Boon storyline continued and they were married in 1963.

During this time, she had a basic faith, she adds in a tone that in no way attempts to belittle those who still have what might be called basic faith. 'It was quite definitely a life that was focused on myself and my worries and what I wanted to do next and what I wanted to avoid. I was just lurching from one emotion to the next, like a lot of people. But eventually I decided that since I believed in God and Christ I would try to live according to Christ's laws.'

An important stage in Elizabeth's spiritual journey took place during a year when she became quite ill and was unable to go out much. 'I read a lot and prayed more and first met Christ in prayer. It didn't convert me because I was already converted to faith. But it converted me to more prayer; more sincere repentance.'

When they moved to Manchester after Kin obtained a job as a registrar at a local hospital Elizabeth's questions about Christianity became more urgent. She was praying daily, reading some of the great Christian thinkers and, by now, going to Mass. In the end, she concluded that the Church Christ had founded through the apostles was the Catholic Church. On a wet night in Manchester in 1968 she was received into the Catholic Church at the Church of the Holy Name, Manchester. 'I didn't have any strong views about anything except that this was the Church that Christ had founded. I was thrilled with the truth I found within it. I hardly knew any Catholics. I knew a Catholic family when I was a child and they were very kind and very loving. But I had been told terrible things about Catholicism.'

The family moved to Harpenden in 1971 after Kin took a job based in hospitals in St Albans and Luton. Elizabeth's painting career began to flourish. Exhibitions at the Royal Academy and other major London galleries led to a regular flow of commissions. She was also a founder member of The Society of Botanical Artists. She was, she concludes, 'a steady working artist' as well as a mother of three children.

One of everyone's worst nightmares happened to Elizabeth in 1988. Two men burst into her home, dragged her around the floor with a knife at her throat, threatened her daughter Mary and fled with most of the family valuables. Understandably, it's still a painful incident for Elizabeth to talk about. 'It was horrific. I think they call it a defining moment. It gave me a great insight into what Christ must have felt in Gethsemane. But I don't want to say any more about it.' From the look in her eyes I can see this is still a painful incident for her to talk about.

Her relationship with Christ continued to deepen through the regular messages, but, she says honestly, for a number of years it was difficult to share them with Kin, who had expressed little interest in Catholicism. However, in 1998 Kin was received into the Church, and he now pays for the publication of Elizabeth's books.

In 1994 she stopped her commercial work and decided to paint images of prayer. She studied colour theory from a book at home and took on board a lot of the ideas of Johannes Itten. 'It was a bit like learning musical harmony. It meant I was more in control of the colour.' She then began a series of paintings of the Mass and incorporated into them images that had been given to her in prayer over the years. She exhibited at Westminster Cathedral in 1992 and then a couple of years later at the Bar Convent Museum, York.

She talks animatedly about there being just a little corner of the Church on earth and says that the people in Purgatory and Heaven are as close as our relatives. Indeed, this is a major theme of her paintings and one that stops you in your tracks. As Catholics, we pay lip service to the doctrine of the communion of saints. But how many of us have ever really thought what that means? How many of us really believe that the material world exists in parallel with an invisible spiritual world of grace and divine love that is just as real?

While committed to ecumenism, and involved in ecumenical activities in Harpenden, she warns against trying to paper over the cracks in an attempt to present an image of unity that doesn't exist. 'At the moment we have some people who put themselves forward as Christian leaders who will say you can have abortions. Others say you can't. Some say if your marriage has failed go and marry someone else. Others say no, that would be adultery. I think everyone deserves to know who is preaching what Christ taught.

'We should say to everyone in the world: love God and love your neighbour. But we know that the Church has always said, "You can't do this by your own power." We need the sacraments. Christ changes us from the inside. Anglicans, Methodists, Quakers, they all need the sacraments. I'm not saying people can't live good lives outside the Church. The Church herself says that those who are already baptised are in partial communion with us. But because we love them we want to offer them the fullness of what the Church has got.'

I mention to her a story I came across the week before on the Internet. An entire, largely black, Pentecostal congregation in the USA had voted to follow their pastor into the Catholic Church. The pastor had wondered why there were 28,000 different Christian denominations in the USA. Eventually his reading and prayer led him to the realisation that the Catholic Church was the Church founded by Christ. Why, I wonder, are there so many churches? And why haven't more sincere, committed, prayerful Protestants reached the same conclusion as herself and the Pentecostal pastor?

From the expression on her face this is clearly a subject about which she has much to say. 'God has lots of ways of speaking to us. He can speak to us in prayer but as we know it is easy to go wrong. The other way God speaks is through the Catholic Church. It's like a big cathedral in the middle of the world. I found it. Everyone who really hunts for the Church that Christ founded can find it. Only some people haven't started the hunt because they are happy with what they have got, or they haven't got puzzled by the big questions, or might have met some Catholics who have really put them off.'

This leads us neatly to the Bible and the accusation some people put that the God of the New Testament is incompatible with the God of the Old Testament. Marcion, in the second century, had held this view and attracted many followers until his excommunication. The conquest of the Promised Land by Joshua, for example, was as brutal and ruthless as any modern military campaign. One Catholic academic had suggested in a book that the Bible has been used to support colonialism and that it was hard to refute claims that, on occasions in the stories of the Old Testament, God seems to encourage and endorse genocide and xenophobia.

Elizabeth will have none of it, though before replying to the question she stresses that she is not a Biblical scholar. 'The Church wants us to approach the books of the Bible through the mind of the author, so that we get a sense of what he wanted to tell us about God. But the picture given in the whole of the Old Testament is of a real and living God progressively revealing himself to a specific people on earth. In other words, taking them from polytheism to the knowledge, through Abraham specifically, that he was one. That there was only one God and that he wanted them to worship, lead a moral life and have religious rituals. He led them gradually to be a prayerful, holy and moral people. He made covenants with them. They kept breaking these covenants. Lots of the stories in the Bible about God are seen through the eyes of aggressive people. His whole message is that he exists, he cares tremendously and its very important for our happiness that we are holy like him. And to be holy we must keep his laws. It's all a preparation for Christ.'

After a pause, she continues. 'He's not a God that loves a whole people, like in the way a headmaster might love his school but without loving the individuals. God is mad about every one of us. Everything we do counts in his sight. As long as we are on this earth we can't possibly go away from God. He's holding in existence stones and worms, birds and everyone on earth.'

In 1985, travelling alone, she made her first trip to the Holy Land, a part of the world, where, in the crucible of politics and religious fundamentalism, some suggest your faith can either be increased or destroyed. 'When I got back I analysed it all. I was so thrilled to be there, to see the holy places. I know that they are not all supposed to be authentic but nevertheless this was Jesus' country. These were the hills he saw in Galilee and that was the lake he sailed on. I realised when I got back that the visit hadn't increased my faith. I don't think it does. If one believes in God then seeing stones and buildings doesn't increase that. But it does make things come alive. When I heard the Gospel the following Sunday in church and the priest mentioned Bethany I no longer had a blank in my head. I could see the road. All those words that I had remembered since I was a toddler: Galilee, Zaccheus, fig tree, I knew what they meant. You can still love Christ and love the Church without ever going to the Holy Land but it's something one ought to do if you can. With any person you love, you want to see where they were born, don't you?'

For many Christians prayer can be difficult. Dryness, boredom and distractions, and feelings of unworthiness can soon set in. The crucial thing, urges Elizabeth, is to persevere. 'How we live our everyday life defines what sort of relationship we have with God in prayer. Oh, this is so important ...' She halts, as if momentarily gripped by excitement, and then continues in an earnest voice: 'The minute we decide to pray to God regularly, even if it's difficult, we will meet God. I don't mean with visions or voices. We will be in contact with him. It's as though a door within us opens a little. And we can choose to let that door open wider if we're honest with him in prayer and willing to give up wrong-doing. When his light shines in our souls it shines on all the bits we are ashamed of. He does this not to make us feel bad but to show us how we can change. But we do feel bad because we are ashamed of being seen as we really are. What we need to believe is that all the time he is loving us. But if we're brave and accept his help and give up these wrong things than that shame goes. That's what prayer's for and that's what Confession's for.

'In the dark years God began teaching me by infused knowledge, which is wordless. I didn't know what was happening and I didn't write about it for years. After that experience of Christ, the spiritual marriage, he started speaking to me in holy communion. And about two or three years after that, he led me to meet the Father in prayer. And he teaches me in a different way. And then the Lord showed me at certain times that it is the Holy Spirit that teaches me. Although when one teaches you the Holy Trinity is at work.'

Elizabeth's face lights up when I ask her what it was like to watch one of her sons being ordained. She explains that, having studied in Oxford, Cambridge and Rome, Stephen was expecting a lot of friends for his ordination in 1998, so a video screen was erected in the Anglican church next door to cope with the overflow. 'It was a little bit of heaven. The local Anglican rector said we could use his church. The wonderful thing that Cardinal Hume agreed to was that a procession would start in the Anglican church, the ordination would take place in Our Lady of Lourdes, and then the procession would return to the Anglican church. It was a little bit like these Oriental feasts that go on for days. First we had the day of the ordination. Then we had the first Mass for his family and friends. Then the day after it was the first Mass for the parish. Every day I was waking up and thinking this is so wonderful! I could hardly believe it, especially when I looked back to the horrible wet night when I came into the church as a convert, all by myself. I had two complete strangers as my sponsors. To be in a church with my husband next to me, my children all Catholics and one of them being made a priest ... I was ... just bowled over by the goodness of God really as well as all the excitement. We put such limits on him. We think he's a bit stingy like us and that he'll dole out a bit of happiness if we pull our socks up.'

It is this message of God's goodness and faithfulness with which Radiant Light aims to revitalise the Church, she says. Around 100 people turned up at its first conference, in 1999. 'Our Lord has told me more about this than I can tell you. It's sometimes said today that there are no easy answers, and this is often said about very straightforward things the Church teaches. We do have answers to all the big things that concern us.'

Before I leave, she shows me her studio – a filled-in porch full of jars of paint brushes and sketches scattered over a desk – and she then leads me into an elegant room where a dozen or so of her stunning paintings of the Mass are stood on the floor. Resting on her stick she looks me in the eye and says gently and with complete conviction, 'One thing God wants me to say to people is never, ever give up. Never give up on him and never give up on the Church. Just keep hanging on in there.'

The Political Journalist

'Now, I've nothing against women playing a very full role in the Church. I'm sure that many of the women who have been ordained in the Anglican Church are much better Christians than I am. But the idea that a middle-class body like the General Synod should just bow to political correctness rather than the collective wisdom of the apostolic Church went totally against the grain with me.'

In his halting, lugubrious voice, rising and falling in the manner of a train shunting in a goods yard, Sir George Gardiner is recalling why he felt compelled to leave the Church of England in 1994 and, like fellow Conservative politicians Ann Widdecombe and John Gummer, seek admission to the Catholic Church. To refresh his memory he is scanning an article he wrote in the *Sunday Express* at the time. Here, he acknowledged the spiritual comfort the Church of England had provided: the choral tradition, the 1662 Book of Common Prayer and the King James Bible. Yet he began to feel that the Church of England was placing social issues before concern for spiritual salvation. He cites a sermon by Bishop Mark Santer in which the current reforms of the Health Service were described as un-Christian. For Sir George this might have come from a Labour Party spokesman. And then in 1994 came the General Synod's decision to allow women to be priests and subsequently his decision to jump ship and join 'the Roman Church'.

He's sitting opposite me in his Edwardian terraced house in a tree-lined street on the borders of Clapham Junction and Wandsworth. Westminster, where George has spent much of his working life, is a short bus ride away, while nearby Wandsworth Common provides a generous splash of greenery amidst the rather gritty urban landscape. Like many successful people in the capital, Sir George has a bolt hole in the country where he spends most weekends. In his case, it's a house in Poole, Dorset.

Dressed in blue trousers and an unbuttoned olive green cardigan, the trademark thick glasses he wore during his twenty-three years as a Conservative backbencher have gone, giving him a more vulnerable, less authoritarian, appearance. Above the fireplace is a large mirror. A display of china is softly lit, not unlike a cupboard of a Bond Street shop. Only a copy of the *Daily Mail* on the biscuit-coloured settee disturbs the air of this being a guest room rather than a living room.

A thin man with a gaunt face and hooded eyes, he was once described as 'the Angel of Death' by Ian Aitken, former political editor of the *Guardian*. Former MP Julian Critchley once wrote: 'Sir George is like a sinister figure with a taste for conspiracy. Were all the world a stage, he would be played by Vincent Price.' Given that Sir George quotes these descriptions in the opening chapter of his political memoirs *A Bastard's Tale*, he's clearly not offended by them. In fact, he probably finds them quite amusing.

Born in 1935 in Witham, Essex, he grew up in what he says were 'fairly straitened circumstances'. He spent the early years of his childhood in Storrington, Sussex. His father was a gasworks manager who, in 1943, moved to Maldon, Essex, to manage a larger plant. There, he met and fell in love with a school teacher. After an acrimonious divorce, Sir George's mother then moved to Hythe in Kent to be near her sister. Unable to find work as a bookkeeper, her profession before marriage, she resorted to working as a waitress in a local tearoom to make ends meet. Apart from a Christmas shopping trip to London and a supply of chocolate rations through the post, Sir George had no further contact with his father, who died a few years later.

Despite this upheaval and the absence of his father, Sir George did well at Harvey Grammar School in Folkestone and won a place to read politics, philosophy and economics at Balliol College, Oxford, for which he received a state scholarship. Aside from attending occasional services at a Congregational church in Hythe, Christianity played only a small role in his life up to this point. It was politics which had fired his young imagination. At fifteen he was a member of Hythe Young Conservatives and would turn up at school wearing the party rosette.

Before he could take his place at Oxford, he had to complete his National Service. He was conscripted to the Royal Army Service Corps, given a job as a clerk, and posted to a barracks in Aldershot. Here he trained as a tester, invigilating and marking intelligence and aptitude tests for recruits to determine in which trade category they should be placed. Promotion to sergeant followed along with an attachment to the Royal Pioneer Corps in Gresford, North Wales.

He says his two years in the army not only made him more mature, but they also enabled him to save £100 to cushion his first year at Oxford. Arriving at Balliol in 1955, wandering through the quadrangles and hidden gardens and soaking up the atmosphere of learning that had produced thirteen out of nineteen cabinet ministers of Anthony Eden's government of the time, he sensed a new and exciting life beginning. He soon became a leading light in the Oxford University Conservative Association. His contemporaries included Kenneth Baker, with whom he lodged for a while, Bryan Walden, Paul Channon and Peter Brook.

'In those days, of course, you bought a card for the term and joined all the parties. When I began in politics it was almost devoid of ideology. There was so little really separating the parties. Okay, nationalisation, yes. But the

Tories had accepted almost all the Atlee reforms, the health service and all the rest,' he recalls.

During his first year, he decided to be confirmed into the Church of England. He had, however, read a series of Catholic Truth Society booklets about Catholicism, but, in the end, felt that he was better suited as an Anglican. 'I very quickly found that I felt most comfortable in the high Anglo-Catholic church and went regularly to a sung Mass which was all "smells and bells", although I sometimes attended services at Pusey House.'

He walked out of Oxford with a first, and then through the doors of the *Bristol Evening Post* as a trainee reporter. He was sent to work in the Stroud branch office, where, driving through the Gloucestershire valleys in his first car, a 1930s Austin convertible, he covered everything from court cases to village flower shows. What he calls 'a memorable drinking friendship' was formed with Laurie Lee, who had then just published *Cider with Rosie*. This involvement in 'the sordid and the sublime' is, he says, excellent training for a career in politics. During this period, he also got married, to Juliet.

When the *Post* took over the *Western Daily Press* he became a sub-editor and then in 1964 was appointed political correspondent and sent to London. He had achieved a dream and was now working at the heart of politics. He and Juliet moved to a house in Blackheath and Sir George became an occasional worshipper at the Anglican church on the Heath. Soon after, he joined the political staff of Thomson Regional Newspapers, who then owned *The Sunday Times*. Before long, he was named the deputy political correspondent of the *The Sunday Times*.

But feeling he wanted to shape politics rather than just report on them, in 1970 he stood as the Conservative candidate for Coventry South, but failed to get in. Four years later he was elected as MP for Reigate and so began twenty-three years as a backbencher and a loyal Thatcherite. He continued his journalism, which by now was quite lucrative, writing regularly for the *Sunday*

Express, *Daily Mail* and other papers on the right.

His marriage to Juliet broke up in 1980 due to 'growing incompatibility'. 'By contrast with my mother's divorce I suppose my divorce from Juliet was as amicable as it could be,' he concludes, clearing his throat. 'Our concern all the time, of course, was for our three children. And we came to an arrangement that on alternate weekends we would have use of the family home. I've maintained contact with Juliet and we occasionally meet for a drink.' He has since remarried, to Helen, now the chairman of the Surrey Ambulance Service Trust, whom he had first met when she was on the committee that selected him for Reigate.

Sensing a gulf between himself and a Church of England leadership who were, he believed, replacing the spiritual message of Christianity with a political one, he began to contemplate becoming a Catholic. 'I knew Ann Widdecombe, who had already become a Catholic, so I asked her how do you set about it. "Oh! she said, you need to go and see Fr Seed."' But Sir George waited about three months before phoning Fr Seed. He wanted to make sure that he was making the right decision.

'I thought there would be a difficulty in accepting me into the Church as I was divorced as was my present wife,' he continues, folding his arms across his chest. 'Our previous marriages were perfectly correct in terms of civil law but they were not recognised under canon law. It transpired that my first wife had been baptised a Roman Catholic. Her mother was Italian. And my first wife's former husband was also baptised a Roman Catholic.'

Did he have any theological difficulties when he met Fr Michael for those regular talks? 'No ... No.' He pauses for what seems an eternity. 'I suppose I'd become in attitude so close that none of the theology came as a surprise to me. I've been very happy in the Roman Church since. I occasionally, though very rarely, get to High Mass in the Cathedral.

'What's come as a bit of a surprise to me is how varied practice is within the standard form of the Mass. You have things that are not far from the happy clappy Anglican tradition and then the very high proper Latin Mass. The church I go to in Bournemouth, for example, offers both the bread and the wine to the congregation, whereas here, in the church down the road, it's just the host. As a former Anglican, the thing I miss most is not having the host and wine together. Ann Widdecombe told me she feels the same way.'

He was received into the Church by Fr Michael Seed at the Church of the Sacred Heart in Horseferry Road, close to Westminster Cathedral, in 1994. He became another 'Seedling', or as Fr Michael himself says in his usual wry manner 'a convertible'. His sponsors were Ann Widdecombe and a family friend who was a member of the Latin Mass Society. 'I really felt I was back home,' he says. His and Helen's marriages were also convalidated.

He hasn't joined any Catholic organisations since his conversion and wonders aloud that perhaps he should. However, he meets some Catholic MP when he occasionally goes to Mass in the crypt chapel of St Mary Undercroft in Westminster. 'That of course, is the chapel for the House of Commons. Nowadays, thankfully, it is available to the Roman Church. Mainly staff go, but I often bump into David Alton, John Gummer and Kevin McNamara there.'

His political career came off the rails in a very public clash over Europe with John Major and he lost his seat at the 1997 General Election. 'When I was an MP I was one of that sturdy bunch of Maastricht rebels. Later, I fell out in quite a major way with John Major.' He gives a chuckle followed by the characteristic long pause. 'An attempt was made in Reigate to deselect me, which I fought off. But there was still a band there who were clearly not satisfied with the outcome. I then wrote an article in the *Sunday Express* that was very critical of John Major. The illustration was a mock-up, a fake photograph if you like, which showed John Major as a kind of puppet sitting on the knee of Kenneth Clark. This was the excuse for a further attempt to deselect me. This time I did not have the support of Central Office. And I lost. I took it to the High Court but lost there too. It was getting very close to the election. I decided that if I was going down, I would go down fighting, so I stood as the Referendum Party candidate for Reigate. I had the predictable result. I think I got 11% of the vote.'

Another lengthy pause. 'I never left the Conservative Party, although I resigned the whip. I was for one week the only Member of Parliament the Referendum Party has ever had. Now I'm a member of the Battersea Conservative Association. I still do a lot with Conservative Way Forward, which I helped to found. I help with local elections, that sort of thing.'

When I ask him if he sees much of Margaret Thatcher nowadays he tells me he is to have tea with her the following week. 'I'm a big fan of hers.' So what does he like about her? 'Oh, her convictions. She's a conviction politician.' Sir George wrote the first biography of Margaret Thatcher, but he has to share this distinction with another journalist who also published a biography of her on the same day.

Does he miss being an MP? 'Not really. Remember I had one spell in opposition. Being in opposition's not nice, especially when you are such a weak opposition, numerically, as they are now. My sort of politics was very much behind-the-scenes stuff. It was back bench pressure.'

He clears his throat again when I ask him how he spends his time and disappears into the kitchen to get a glass of water, asking me if I would like another cup of coffee as he reaches the door. I know he's writing a work of fiction because half-an-hour before, I overheard him talking about this to a friend on the telephone. No publisher yet. But his agent is optimistic, he cheerily remarks.

An important part of his life today is his work for The Children's Trust. The Children's Trust began as Tadworth Court Children's Hospital, which was a country offshoot of Great Ormond Street. 'While I was a member of parliament Great Ormond Street wanted to close it because they had some financial difficulties. They wanted to relocate some of the patients to another NHS hospital and sell off this very big site. I began a campaign to save it. I was helped a lot by the Cystic Fibrosis Trust, but also, and much more to the point, by the body that was then called the Spastic Society. And with the Spastic Society I helped to put together a rescue plan.'

The then Secretary of State, Norman Fowler, agreed to reprieve the hospital, divorce it from Great Ormond Street, divide the site, sell off part of it for housing and allow a new charity, the Children's Trust, to run the hospital.

Since a heart by-pass operation at the Westminster Hospital in 1982 he has had a renewed sense of gratitude to God for life, he says. 'I can honestly say – and I know it sounds presumptuous – that I never felt any fear of death. Since then, every morning when I've woken up I've had this feeling, "Thank God, I'm here to live another day; to make the most of it; enjoy it." I suppose it's a form of prayer in a way. Not the conventional form, but a feeling of gratitude each morning even if you're a bit under the weather for some reason.'

He's proud of the successful careers his three children from his first marriage have made for themselves. Alexander is an executive producer for London Weekend Television, currently working on a documentary about the Hesseltine years. Sophie is an independent TV producer whose credits include Eureka Street. And Sebastian is a barrister.

There are times, he believes, when politicians must stand up for their faith, and times when Church leaders should stand up for their beliefs. He praises Cardinal Winning's robust stand on issues such as abortion and protecting children from homosexual influences. 'I think it right that politicians should seek to give expression to their religious faith by what they do in politics. But it becomes very hard for a Conservative who is a devout member of the Church of England to read some of the stuff its bishops spout all the time with the implication that they, as Conservatives, are somehow failing in their duty to God. I don't see why one party should be more virtuous in the eyes of God than any other.'

He becomes more thoughtful and cups his hand to his face. 'The one great regret – and it's a sin I've not properly atoned for – I have, is that during my days as an MP I consistently voted against efforts by David Alton and others to amend David Steele's Abortion Act. It wasn't until I joined the Roman Church that I realised what a sin being party to that was.'

He then remembers something and leaves the room. When he returns he tells me he was looking for a photo of his wife with the Pope. But, he adds, it must be at the Poole House.

'In those days there was a successful company at Gatwick called Air Europe. They began with charter flights but then developed scheduled services to European capitals. They had an inaugural flight to Rome. The public relations adviser to the company was a devout Catholic, Nirj Deva, a Mauritian who went on to become MP for Hammersmith and is now an MEP for London. He assembled a whole lot of MPs and their wives to go on this flight. At the last moment Nirj managed to secure us an audience with his Holiness the Pope. So we met Pope John Paul II, were individually presented to him and pictures were taken. I've lost my picture but my wife had hers framed. She was very, very impressed by him.' Helen, also a former Anglican, has also now been received into the Catholic Church.

He thinks for a moment and uncrosses his legs. 'Now, I'm not saying that that was in any way relevant to my conversion. It wasn't. But, there is something about the man. Very gentle and very impressive. You can understand why he was made Pope. Put it this way: it undoubtedly increased my respect for the Roman Church long before I contemplated joining it.'

The Philosopher

Paul Williams is Professor of Indian and Tibetan Philosophy and Head of the Department of Theology and Religion at the University of Bristol. This chapter is taken from material in his forthcoming book on his conversion, due to be published by Continuum/T & T Clark in 2001. He was received into the Catholic Church at Clifton Cathedral, Bristol, at Easter 2000.

I wasn't always a Buddhist. As far as I recall our immediate family was not particularly religious, although on our father's side there were practising Anglicans and relatives had been Anglican clergy. On our mother's side I do not remember any especial interest in religion. I heard once that our maternal grandmother had said she would be a Buddhist if she were anything at all. I discovered fairly recently that in fact our maternal grandfather's family had been Roman Catholic, although he had abandoned the faith.

I am not sure why, but for some reason when I was really quite young I joined the local Anglican church choir at Pinhoe near Exeter. I loved singing church music. I still remember the village church, which dated back to Saxon times. My younger brother Gerald and I took our religion terribly seriously. We would sit up in bed having theological discussions, our heads respectfully nodding like Pelham puppets every time we mentioned the name of Jesus. I sometimes wondered whether I might not eventually become a Church of England vicar. As far as I recall the only society I joined at my secondary school was the Christian Union. I remember even then feeling myself different from others in taking Christianity so seriously. Oh, but I was different! For I had walked and spoken with Jesus in the Garden. I remember distinctly dreaming at about this time that I walked and talked with Jesus. Jesus was, of course, in white. The Garden was, of course, green. I do not remember what we said. I like to think he was sending me on my path through life, away from the Garden into adolescence and adulthood – never really to leave him, and to return in his own good time. When I have forgotten so much about my childhood, that remains vividly with me still. Was the philosopher Hobbes right when he said that the man who thinks that God spoke to him in a dream merely dreamed that God spoke to him?

Our mother died when I was twelve or thirteen – I forget which exactly. On our mother's death we eventually moved to Westgate-on-Sea in Kent, and after accompanying our father in a brief flirtation with Christian Science I rejoined the local Anglican church choir. I sometimes sang solo, and in addition took part in a folk singing group outside the church context. My two brothers were also in the choir, and in time I became head chorister. Unfortunately my voice broke rather early and, since I was thought to be too young to be a bass, as far as I recall I spent my entire time as head chorister miming. This perhaps gave me an early taste of the buff necessary for an academic career.

At the appropriate age in the early 1960s I was confirmed in the Anglican Church by the Bishop of Dover. I became a server at Holy Communion. One day Gerald brought home a book on yoga from the local library. Thus started my interest in Indian thought. As the 1960s wore on I became involved in the lifestyle and all the normal things that teenage boys get up to. As public examinations loomed larger, I left the choir, ceased to be a server, and lost contact with the Church. I grew long hair, and dressed strangely. I went to the University of Sussex to read for a degree in Philosophy and Religion in the School of African and Asian Studies, since that way as a philosophy student I could also study Indian philosophy for my degree. I became very involved with Maharishi Mahesh Yogi's Transcendental Meditation, which was popular at that time, but eventually I became bored and frustrated with what seemed to me to be its superficiality and distortion of Indian thought and ideas.

I subsequently took my doctorate in Buddhist philosophy at the University of Oxford. One reason for opting for Buddhism was that it meant I would not be restricted entirely to Indian thought if ever I decided to move over to, say Tibetan or Chinese philosophy. In fact much of my recent work, as it turned out, has been in Tibetan. During my early days at Oxford I recall drinking gin and tonics one New Year's Eve with R. C. Zaehner, himself a Catholic convert and the Spalding Professor of Eastern Religion and Ethics. An eccentric character who managed to set fire to his rooms at All Souls College with a cigarette, Zaehner died long before the 1970s had finished. I still remember on that New Year's Eve his Aristotelian (or maybe Augustinian) toast: 'May you become what you always were.'

By about 1970-ish I was already beginning to think of myself as a Buddhist. I finally 'Took Refuge', formally becoming a Buddhist in the Tibetan tradition. That was after a weekend on Buddhist thought given by Ven. Geshe Damcho Yonten, Spiritual Director of the Lam Rim Buddhist Centre, which is on the borders of Wales. It was, I think, 1978. I had just finished my doctorate. Our father had died, still quite young, the previous year. When I found myself teaching at the nearby University of Bristol in the early 1980s I re-established contact with the Lam Rim Centre, setting up with others a group in Bristol that also now has its own Dharma (Buddhist) Centre. I became involved in occasional teaching within the context of practising Buddhism at both Buddhist centres, and I was invited to be a trustee of the Lam Rim Centre. As well as my academic work in Buddhist philosophy I wrote and spoke as a Tibetan Buddhist on television, the radio and at conferences. I took part in public and private dialogue with Christians, including Hans Kung and Raimundo Panikkar. My dialogues with both of these have been published. Perhaps one day I shall debate with Kung again, this time from a very different position.

One's past, especially one's early conceptual outlook, cannot be easily avoided. I remember feeling very uncomfortable when one of my fellow Buddhists teased me with having broken my religious vows made to the Bishop of Dover at my confirmation. It was true. I had broken my vows. I had indeed made promises. Once I was interviewed by the well-known psychiatrist Anthony Clare for a television programme on Buddhism in Britain. He asked me whether, since I worked in the study of religions, I had considered carefully the claims of each religion before finally choosing Buddhism. He had touched a sensitive point. Had I really considered carefully the claims of even Christianity, the religion I was baptised and confirmed into? Now, I had problems with the notion of a creator God, particularly in the light of evil. But I also knew that many intelligent people were nevertheless able to be Christians, including some people I much admired. Was I certain that I could not be a Christian, that my rejection of Christianity was well founded? Could I stake my (eternal) life on it? Or had I simply drifted away from Christianity, and into Buddhism, because I had a professional interest in the subject and to be a Buddhist was fashionable and my knowledge of the subject flattered me?

That wasn't all. When chanting Tibetan I sometimes felt distinctly unhappy when chanting the Tibetan prefix *rjes su*, pronounced *jesu*, as if in some sense committing blasphemy in that environment, recalling choices previously made, commitments gone back on, and perhaps decisions yet to come. It sounds silly, I know. But that is how I sometimes felt. I once attended a series of workshops on Jung's psychology and Tibetan Buddhism. We were given various guided visualisations, and I found that whenever I was asked to visualise a peaceful scene I always tended to see the classic English countryside with a medieval church. I still loved visiting cathedrals and country churches. I remember a strong feeling when turning up at a church on a Sunday afternoon, that I was looking in at the scene of a party after all the guests had departed. Deep down I wanted to be part of it, yet I could only bring myself to view the setting. I was invited, yet I always arrived too late. Once when I was in Dharamsala, the north Indian hill station where the Dalai Lama lives, I remember telling a young woman that she didn't need to come all the way to India to find spirituality. She could find it back home in Europe. Had she tried Christian meditation? She seemed surprised, and, I think, very relieved. But it was not what she had expected me to say.

I always liked Catholics. I used to say that any tradition that produced St Thomas Aquinas must have something to be said for it. I remember trying to read works on Aquinas in the cloisters of Canterbury Cathedral while still at school. And since Vatican II the Catholics had seemed to me, rightly or wrongly, to be by far the most open and understanding of the Christian traditions I was familiar with, while still preserving a fair degree of doctrinal and moral clarity. A combination of openness and the rich Catholic intellectual and spiritual tradition was very tempting. Pity about the problems with God though.

G. K. Chesterton has commented somewhere that usually when a Westerner converts to a non-Christian religion they never really convert to that religion at all. All they really convert to is Christianity minus the parts of Christianity they find unpalatable. If we look at Western Buddhists, and so-called Western Buddhism, we regularly find that it is a form of Christianity stripped of the parts that post-Christians find so difficult to accept.

Buddhism in the way it is presented to so many Western practitioners is of course pre-eminently a religion of kindness and compassion to others. Western Buddhists are keen to emphasise that Buddhism is not world negating, but implies one way or another direct action in the world to benefit all sentient beings. There is a tendency in Western Buddhism to push the laity and the option of social engagement to the ideological forefront. This care is to be for all *sentient* beings, not just human beings. It includes wiggly worms as much as humans. And Western Buddhism as a religion also has a major advantage over Christianity. It is liberated from the idea of a creator God. It plays down the role of faith, which, as it is employed by Christians, Buddhists always seem to think of as 'blind faith', and stresses direct personal experience.

What this Buddhism is all about is in its widest sense *positive experiences*. 'We all want to be happy and avoid suffering,' the Dalai Lama regularly begins his talks. Buddhism is the supreme way to do this. Buddhism (as thus popularly understood by its Western enthusiasts) leads to happiness in day to day life, feelings of harmony, feelings of love and compassion, insight into reality, and *mystical experiences* through meditation. All this is without requiring, like Christianity, an extensive, and apparently bizarre, belief system and regular attendance at communal ritual. Even a belief in rebirth is often said to be unessential. We can be confident also that Buddhism is in conformity with the latest discoveries of science. In fact, Western Buddhism is a religion of self-development, 'self-empowerment'. Any moral code tends to be explained as 'rules of training' to be adopted for their *usefulness* in one's day-to-day life and spiritual training, not because they are imposed by an external authority, particularly a patriarchal authority like God. Western Buddhism involves preeminently meditation, which has direct psychological benefits. Buddhist meditation is not like prayer, or a church service. It need not involve being with others, or God as an Other. And it is to be judged through the pleasant sensations of calm, relaxation, loving feelings, and so on that it engenders. In becoming a Buddhist one can centre a whole religion on practical experiences deriving from meditation, on direct and obvious personal *returns.*

Such a reading of Buddhism portrays it as a religious tradition attractive to the contemporary Western world and post-modern individualism. It is a world with an interest in the exotic, good returns for investment, a craving for the 'feel good factor' as well as deep experiences, the moulding of an elite, superior not just in wealth or luxury but also in wisdom. It is all bundled together as 'spirituality'. The New Age has become a way of fending off old age. Perhaps also we are impressed by the Dalai Lama, or by other Buddhists we meet. Everyone likes Tibetans. But I am not sure, however, if all this is a basis for genuine conversion to authentic Buddhism. In my own case, I now think I was a Buddhist by default, not by conviction. Eventually I returned to see whether the problems I feared in Christianity were really the problems I thought they were.

In *The Everlasting Man* G. K. Chesterton tells how he once failed to write a story. It would have been, he thought, the best story he had ever written had he done so. It would have been about a boy who lived in a farm cottage on the slope of a valley. One day the boy sets off to find some valuable object in the landscape, perhaps a grave and effigy of a great giant. Eventually he looks back and sees in the distance below him his little cottage. There he 'saw that his own farm and kitchen garden, shining flat on the hillside like the colours and quarterings of a shield, were but parts of some such gigantic figure, on which he had always lived, but which was too large and close to be seen.' We travel a long way to try to find something of great value. It is only from that distance that we can see we really had our treasure all along. It was all around us. It was not where we were going but where we came from. Why did we fail to see it? Why didn't we realise the surprise we would have when we found out where it really was? But we needed the distance. We needed to be elsewhere in order to see it. We failed to discern the great treasure when it was but our familiar surroundings, for it was too close to us. Such has been my journey as well.

Yet unlike Chesterton's great figure in the landscape, God is not inert. He is not dead. It seems He followed me. I think I knew it all along. I could hear the footsteps. And I ran. Yet it now seems clear I kept looking back half in fear and half in hope, drawn by that from which I ran. Why does God chase us like that? Why will He not let us go? As St Augustine said, 'The thought of you stirs (Man) so deeply that he cannot be content unless he praises you, because you made us for yourself and our hearts find no peace until they rest in you.'

I have never seen my academic study as divorced from the religio-philosophical quest for understanding. Absolutely central to my growing unease with Buddhist affiliation was my paper 'Altruism and rebirth'. It was while working on that paper that, for the first time, I think I truly appreciated the significance of the central, and it seems to me correct, Buddhist claim that with reincarnation the rebirth could not be said to be the *same person* as the one who died. I began to think that if Buddhism were correct then unless I attained enlightenment or something like it in this life *I* – Williams, the person I am – would have no hope. For actually the rebirth of Williams that follows from my not attaining enlightenment could not possibly be the same person as Williams. Clearly I was not going to attain enlightenment in this life. So I, and I suspect all my friends and family, must have *in themselves* finally no hope. Not only that. Actually from a Buddhist perspective in the scale of infinite time and infinite rebirths the significance of each of us as such, as the person we actually are now, converges on nothing. Thus Buddhism for me appeared to be *hope -less.* As St Paul knew so well, Christianity at least offers *hope.*

I remember consciously deciding to switch my perspective, to see what things would look life *if* I saw them as if I thought Christianity were true. In that switch of perspective I now think I invited Christ to return. He came.

My actual conversion to Christianity springs from my conviction that Christianity – indeed Catholicism – is factually, cognitively, *true*. In other words, my interest in Christianity, and my conversion, is bound up with issues of how things are, expressed in philosophical and theological *doctrines*, dogmas. The point is worth making because I have found that failing to appreciate this point can lead to deep misunderstanding. Christians with an interest in Buddhism are often fascinated primarily by Buddhist *meditation*. They are attracted by the richness and depth of Buddhist meditation practices, and keen to learn from Buddhists and find a meeting point in meditation and mystical experience. Thus there can be a tendency to portray doctrinal differences as unessential.

The religions finally meet on the level of meditative – mystical – experience, and it is mystical experience that tells us how things really are. Mystical experience, however, by its very nature is held to be beyond language and non-conceptual, and, it is claimed, it is in the stammering attempts to express such experiences that differences between Buddhism and Christianity occur. Indeed there is sometimes a feeling that inasmuch as the very expression of mystical experience occurs within the conceptual categories most familiar to the meditator, it is those conceptual categories and thus accidental differences of time and place that force misunderstanding and difference.

For all I know, this scenario may be true. But I do not myself hold any of it. Thus the convert from Buddhism to Catholicism can find himself distinctly out of sympathy with a lifelong Catholic with a profound interest in Buddhism and who was perhaps expecting to find a soul mate with a similarity of interests and perspective. Indeed, converts from Christianity to Buddhism often have a deep interest in Buddhist meditation and little interest as such in the very real differences of Buddhist and Christian theology and philosophy, and their crucial importance. If my experience is anything to go by, a convert from

Buddhism to Christianity has a deep interest in Christian philosophy and theology, and little interest *as such* in purported similarities of Buddhist and Christian meditation and their associated experiences. For philosophical and theological niceties are essential to any articulate understanding of how things really are, i.e. truth, and one thing Buddhists and Christians agree is that understanding how things really are is essential to our salvation. Experiences that are said to be non-conceptual and unutterable should be viewed with distinct suspicion – suspicion of their relevance but also of their very coherence.

It is my conviction of the *truth* of Christianity, precisely expressed in its dogmas, that has converted me from Buddhism to Catholicism.

A. For I have come to believe that God exists. The God I hold to exist is God as a necessary being, Creator of all things out of nothing. All other things are created, and as such are of a totally unimaginably different order from God. This God is the sort of God that would be recognisable to Christian orthodoxy as represented by the Catholic tradition of Aquinas.

Buddhists do not hold that such a God exists. Thus I could no longer be a Buddhist.

B. I have also come to believe that Jesus was indeed bodily resurrected from the dead. That is, I believe Jesus genuinely died, the tomb was empty, and Jesus was subsequently, after his real death, physically alive. He had been physically resurrected from the dead. I repeat the word 'physically' because I gather there are those who accept the resurrection yet interpret it differently from what I would call a literal, physical resurrection. Perhaps they take the resurrection as a vision, or as a myth, or as a way of speaking about an understanding that the disciples gained concerning the significance of Jesus's life and death. They do not take it as a literal, physical, bodily resurrection. I understand that scholars working on the resurrection sometimes refer to the sort of literalist approach that I have come to accept by saying that it entails that if someone had possessed a working camera they would have photographed Jesus after the resurrection. Fine. That is what I mean.

Since I believe the resurrection took place, in the sense in which I have defined it, I do not feel I can be any sort of theist apart from a Christian. I cannot be a Muslim, or a mainstream Jew, or a dualist Saivite or Vaisnavite. None of these, as I understand it, accepts the literal physical resurrection of Jesus from the dead. At least, while it may not follow strictly, it seems to me to make more sense to be a Christian if one accepts the resurrection.

C. If I am to be Christian, what sort of Christian? I want to argue that priority has to be given to the Roman Catholic Church. In other words, I need a strong argument *not* to be a Catholic. Since I fail to be convinced by arguments not to be a Catholic I shall be a Catholic. One of my principles here is that on some things – indeed, some very important things – we cannot know what God has actually done short of him telling us. His telling us is a revelation. One form of revelation is Scripture. But God cannot be constrained, and that is only one form of revelation. Another major form of revelation is through the tradition and teaching authority (*magisterium*) of an authoritative Church.

A recurrent theme running through much of my thought on these things has been the philosophical and spiritual dangers of basing religion on what I shall term 'subjectivism', or 'subjectivity'. Subjectivism occurs in systems that give overwhelming primacy to certain sorts of private experiences, sensations, intuitions, or emotions, and seek to base all that is ultimately most valuable in the religious (or other ideological) system on those. It is ultimately in those intuitions or experiences, such as the emotion of feeling saved, feeling one with the universe, seeing God, or the experience of *nirvana*, enlightenment, that the rest of the religion concerned is validated. Thus ultimate authority, or validation, or the goal, is essentially *private*. This can be contrasted with the authority of an external body, revelation through the public words of Scripture (literally understood, if that is possible), or the public pronouncements of an authoritative Church. It seems to me that subjectivism is prone to losing all sense of objectivity of truth. It has a genuine problem in escaping the privacy of experience, and hence solipsism (*the* world itself as nothing more than the world of the flow of *my own* experiences). It thus provides an insufficient base for grounding not only a common world of objective being but also (and therefore) any genuine morality and any spiritual practice apart from self interest. I now think that only in Being Itself, i.e. necessary being, in other words God, can the objectivity of the everyday world be grounded. And correspondingly only in a divinely authorised and hence infallible Church founded on Being Itself can morality and a spiritual liberation which transcends individual self interest be also grounded.

I want to claim that Buddhism has an 'explanatory gap' that, *if it is to be filled at all*, can only be filled with necessary being. Why is there something rather than nothing? And in particular why is there a world in which, among other things, the processes (causation, the so-called law of *karman* etc.) detected by the Buddha are the case? As the Buddhist scriptures (*sutras*) have it: 'Whether Buddhas occur or do not occur, the true way of things (Sanskrit: *dharmata*) remains.' But why? Why is it like that? The *dharmata* is not what we call 'necessarily Existent'. That is, there is no logical *contradiction* in a world in which all things are not like that – no causation, or no causation like that, or the Buddhist path does not lead to liberation etc. Thus the *dharmata*, the true way of things, is contingent. It could have been otherwise. We have a contingent fact or state of affairs, how things happen to be in the actual world, for which we are entitled to ask the reason. 'Surely,' we could urge, 'there must *be* a reason.' Why are things just like that, and not otherwise?

The questions 'Why is there something rather than nothing?', or 'Why is the true way of things *that* way, and not *another* way?' became for me a bit like what Zen Buddhists call a *koan*. They were constant, unavoidable, niggling questions that worried and goaded me, often, I think, against my will, into a different level of understanding, a different vision of the world and our place in it. For as a Buddhist I simply had no answer.

Among the reasons that disposed me to opt for Christianity is its relative optimism. I am not using the term 'optimism' here in any vague sense. What I mean is that for reasons to do with the nature of rebirth, if Buddhism is correct then this life will be the end for me and for all my loved ones. If Buddhism is right, then finally for almost all of us our little lives count for virtually nothing. If Christianity is right, on the other hand, our lives – as the lives of the individual persons we are – are infinitely valuable, and we all have the possibility as the persons we are of unimaginable perfection. In this very specific sense, related to personal survival, potential, and value, I call the Christian scenario 'optimistic'. Relative to that, the scenario of the Buddhist is pessimistic. Of course, if the Buddhist is right in his or her analysis of the nature of things then they can be portrayed as optimistic in that they at least show a way out of the infinite series of miserable rebirths. But the very idea that this is how it is, is pessimistic. If the universe is such that *ultimately* the only thing to do is to escape an infinite series of rebirths, and ultimately to help others to do the same, that is pessimistic.

The optimist has a tendency to live on and in *hope*. Thus in my case the choice to opt for Christianity, even though for all I *know* Buddhism may turn out to be correct, given all that I have said, is based on *hope*. Put frankly, I hope Christianity is true, much more than I could ever say I *hoped* Buddhism were true.

It seems to me, moreover, that the orthodox Christian position on many fundamental issues, at least as represented by the Catholic tradition, and that of the Buddhist are exact opposites. The Christian orients him or herself towards God, the absolutely Other. This orientation is essentially dualistic. The Buddhist does not hold the existence of such a God. In response to this orientation, the Christian sees everything in terms of God and the grace of God. The Christian is acutely aware of his or her own spiritual incapacity. Everything flows from God, a God who is quite Other than His creation even if He is a God who has in Christ entered into creation and, as it were, become part of it. All initiative comes from without. Christianity is all and entirely about God. As such it is not about personal *experiences* at all. The Buddhist thinks in terms of mental transformation, a transformation of the mind from greed, hatred and delusion to their opposites. Thus the orientation of the Buddhist is towards the primacy of certain types of experiences, and key experiences are frequently expressed in terms of non-conceptuality and non-dualism. Buddhism is all about the mind and with a few exceptions in the last analysis the Buddhist brings about his or her own mental transformation. 'Buddhas but point the way,' says one of the Buddhist scriptures.

These and other differences between orthodox Catholic Christianity and Buddhism are differences in *whole orientation*. They are frequently missed in concentrating on details and superficial similarities. Frequently nowadays one suspects a degree of embarrassment, at least on the side of some Christians, at these differences and what follows from them. For what follows is the imperative of *choice*. And in choosing they are absolutely crucial. Of course, on all of these issues debate can take place interminably. But at some point in life one has to make a decision – yes or no? For me one cannot be half a Christian. Christianity demands that one makes a wholehearted commitment. I could not avoid that choice. Realising the choice, realising deep within the *urgency* of the choice – facing it and making it once and for all, even if that involves a gamble, I could not say 'No'. Consequently I had to say 'Yes'. I suppose in the last analysis it was as simple as that. And I am so, so very grateful.

The Student

'When we took the children down to the grotto for the first time it felt really strange. I was excited for the kids, but I didn't get anything from it myself. Then the priest in our group invited me to go down to the grotto with him at night. He told me it was very different. When we arrived there I just broke down in tears. The priest asked me what I was feeling. I told him this was such a special place and that I felt a great weight had been lifted off my shoulders. The problems I'd had at college seemed irrelevant. That was a big turning point. I came back and said to Debbie, the lay chaplain, that I wanted to do the RCIA course and be received into the Catholic Church.'

Twenty-one-year-old Emma Seccombe is reliving the moment in 1997 when she decided to become a Catholic. She was visiting Lourdes for the first time, as a helper with a HCPT (Handicapped Children's Pilgrimage Trust) group from Newport, Gwent, and, like many, she had been deeply touched by the unique spiritual atmosphere that emanates from this little French town, nestling in the Pyrenees, where, in 1858, fourteen-year-old Bernadette Soubirous received visions of the Virgin Mary.

Emma and I are sitting in a bright, comfortable room in the modern Catholic chaplaincy building at St Mary's College, Strawberry Hill, near Twickenham. Situated in a quiet, leafy corner of suburban London, St Mary's is the oldest Catholic college in the UK, established by the Vincentians 150 years ago.

An outgoing and bubbly young woman, she is a sub-warden in her hall of residence and is also very involved in the student union. She has just completed her exams at the end of her final year and is now looking forward to the college ball at the weekend when a funfair will set up specially for the event.

She talks in that quick fire, enthusiastic way of so many confident twenty-somethings. Words such as 'brilliant', 'absolutely' and 'incredible' pepper her sentences, which often end unfinished as a new train of thought takes over.

'In my first year at St Mary's I found life very stressful,' she admits, as she explains what led her, then an agnostic, to go to Lourdes. 'A friend of mine used to go to Mass regularly. One day she invited me to go to Mass with her. She told me it would give me an hour of quiet where I would have time to think. So I agreed and things just seemed to click into place. I came out of the chapel feeling a lot better. I then started going each week, just listening to the gospel and then talking to people about it afterwards. Gradually I began to understand that you couldn't blame God for everything. At high school I had lost my nan on my dad's side as well as the eighteen-month-old baby of another member of my family. I blamed it all on God. I had grown up believing that God controlled everything. I then concluded that there couldn't be a God. How could there be if something like this happened? I just had a very negative view of religion.'

Her childhood in Wimbledon, south London, had been a happy one, with one of the highlights being a fortnight each year in a resort on the Costa Brava, where a family friend owned a bar and restaurant. Her family though, she giggles, is a little bit complicated. Her mother had divorced her first husband, with whom she had had two daughters, remarried and then given birth to Emma. 'My two step-sisters see their dad all the time. And their dad and my dad are very good friends. Both our families have always got on well and there have been no problems.'

An outgoing and energetic child, Emma attended dance classes from the age of three. At the age of thirteen, having appeared on *Opportunity Knocks*, presented by Des O'Connor, she began attending The Young Set performing arts school in Feltham, run by the mother of actress Bonny Langford.

In 1995 she appeared as a member of The Young Set dance group at the Royal Variety Performance at the London Palladium. Rubbing shoulders with stars such as Bruce Forsythe and Celine Dion was an amazing experience, she says. But it was Michael Barrymore who impressed her the most. 'He was the most kind, generous person you could wish to meet. There were over forty of us in the dance group and he made the point of getting to know each of us.'

Her mother, one of eight children born to Irish parents, was a practising Catholic. But her father refused to allow Emma to be baptised a Catholic. So she was baptised into the Church of England.

'Up until I came here the only time I had been to church was for weddings, funerals and christenings,' she says with a casual flick of her blonde hair.

'My dad isn't very religious. He believes in God, but wouldn't go to church. All his family were Church of England. He had this thing about Catholicism and didn't want me to be baptised Catholic. My mum just wanted me baptised so she agreed for me to be baptised into the Church of England.'

Emma attended Ricards Lodge girls school before going on to take her A levels at Esher College. As with many state schools, religion and God were seen as having little part to play in any future life. 'Religion wasn't talked about. When we did RE the big issue was that people hated studying other religions. Christianity would be studied for two weeks but then six weeks would be spent on Buddhism. People would ask, why are we spending six weeks on Buddhism and only two weeks on Christianity? When we did Christianity all the denominations were lumped together so no one had much of an understanding of the differences between them.'

While at Ricards Lodge she volunteered to help out at a summer school for disabled children and instantly fell in love with the work. 'It was absolutely brilliant. I got so much out of it and I knew the kids got so much from me.' She takes a rare pause. 'People say you can either do it or you can't.'

She is also a part-time youth worker, mainly with disadvantaged and disabled children. She tells me that recently the youth club took a group of nine to eleven year olds to the countryside and in the summer she will be running drama workshops. This gives her an opportunity to put some of her dance and drama skills to good use. She also works as a volunteer with the Home to Home scheme, which befriends and supports families with disabled children. This might involve taking children out for a day or having them to stay overnight with her family.

'You work with children who have been abused, for example. And some children can't toilet themselves or bath themselves. It's not always easy and I've had times when I've thought enough is enough and that I don't want to do it any more,' she confesses.

When she decided to study for a degree in drama and sociology she opted for St Mary's College because she knew friends and teachers who had studied there.

Having an interest in helping disabled children, she thought Lourdes sounded intriguing when she was invited to join the Newport HCPT group as a college representative. Nevertheless, knowing little about Catholicism, and knowing that Lourdes was 'very Catholic' she was apprehensive as she waited in the departure lounge at Gatwick Airport.

'I was a bit worried that I might not fit in and that people would be asking me what I was doing there. But when I arrived my first thought was, what a beautiful area. And when I booked into the hotel and met the group, after five minutes with them I felt I had known them for ten years.'

She shakes her head when I ask her to describe Lourdes for someone who hasn't been there. 'It's so hard. When I go and lecture to other colleges about the Simms HCPT group at St Mary's and what we do, it's so hard to explain. Basically it's just a week where you take away children with a variety of disabilities or problems. For example, the child I looked after last year had been sexually abused by a grandparent. The whole of the day is for them. We have daily Mass, do things like the stations of the cross, go into the mountains, visit the museum of the story of Lourdes and the basilicas. At night the helpers go down into the town and spend the night in the cafe and bars. It's a brilliant atmosphere.'

During this week in Lourdes she began discussing Catholicism with a woman in her group, talking late into the night as they walked in the quiet of the grotto. 'With Catholicism I always felt that you either accepted every single thing or you couldn't be a Catholic. She explained to me that it wasn't about having to accept every single thing, but it was about your relationship with God.'

She knew something had happened to her out in Lourdes and when she commenced her second year at St Mary's she made enquiries about doing the RCIA course. But then her mum had a stroke and her grandmother was diagnosed with Alzheimers, so she was away from college a lot. She returned to Lourdes with the same HCPT group the following summer and left feeling even more strongly that she wanted to become a Catholic.

'But I'm glad I waited until this year actually to do the course because it gave me a couple of years to decide that this was definitely what I wanted to do.'

Along with another student, in October 1999 Emma began a six-month RCIA course with Debbie Bhati, the lay chaplain at St Mary's, and was confirmed in the college chapel. In recognition of the special place Lourdes has in her life, she chose Bernadette as her confirmation name.

How has her dad reacted to her becoming a Catholic? 'He's been really supportive. He came along with my mum to my confirmation. He doesn't mind what I choose because I am now old enough to make my own decision. He knows how important it is for me taking children to Lourdes. And he's brilliant with the disabled children I bring home.

'When Debbie asked me how it felt to be confirmed as a Catholic I said to be honest I don't feel my life's going to change because I feel I have been living a Christian life since I came to St Mary's. But I do feel different although I can't explain why.

'As a child, I knew about Jesus through things like nativity plays. Now, I just see how Jesus and God are present everywhere. I can see Him in other people, objects. Every day I know that God and Jesus are with me. At times when I'm feeling pretty low that's what keeps me going. Now I have faith and an understanding of the world, when I read the Bible it makes so much sense. And now I can take examples of what's happened to me or in society and relate back to the stories in the Bible.'

Why does she think so many young people today dismiss religion? 'I think now it's not so much that people aren't religious and that they don't have faith, it's more that they don't practise it much. A lot of people feel that they don't have to prove it by going to church. A lot of the Irish students here don't go to Mass because they were forced to go back home. I believe a lot of people have faith. But I think many Churches don't do much to encourage young people to become involved. There's a view that the Church is restrictive and that you have to be like a saint to be a member. You might look at the rugby lads at college, drinking and going off with women, and think they're not religious. But I believe they are. A lot of people at college know that I have done the RCIA and been confirmed. They say to me that I am so lucky I have made the choice because all my Catholic friends say that they don't remember their confirmation and making the decision to be a Catholic.'

She has decided to stay on at St Mary's to train as a primary school teacher. She adds that after gaining some experience in mainstream education she will move into special needs. Here, she hopes to use all her experience and training in drama.

Clearly, Lourdes has been a major junction in her faith journey. But what is it that makes it so special? 'I don't know. You just go out there and you see all these people who have such faith and you wonder why. But when you go to the grotto yourself you just ... you just know. It's really hard to explain what that feeling is,' she says, searching for the right expression, then adding with a wide smile, 'I've got the bug now.'

The Social Activist

There are turning points in all our lives, though we may only identify them in retrospect. For Dr Ian Linden one such moment occurred while working with the rag-pickers in a Paris suburb in the summer of 1961. That experience introduced him to his future wife and the Catholic Church, and it also enabled him to find his vocation as a campaigner for peace and justice in the Third World.

A tall balding man with a brillo-pad beard, wearing a brown and white striped jacket, white trousers and suede shoes, Ian Linden has been the executive director of the Catholic Institute for International Relations (CIIR) for the last fourteen years.

Located in a former factory, now a complex of business units, CIIR is as little known in some Catholic circles as the quiet corner of north London which it inhabits. Yet it is an organisation with an annual budget of over £4.5 million and a membership of 2,500.

It may have one of those acronyms that are awkward to pronounce but since it was established in 1940, it has become a major, if frequently unnoticed, player in the world of aid, development and human rights. Its work is underpinned by Catholic social teaching which attempts to apply Gospel values to the contemporary world.

CIIR has two main roles: providing professionals to share their skills with agencies in the developing world and attempting to influence the policies of the movers and shakers at local, national and international level. Currently, it employs 130 experienced development workers in projects ranging from agriculture to information technology, in the Caribbean, Latin America, southern Africa and the Middle East. Its team in London carry out research and analysis, organise public meetings and briefings for politicians, the media, other agencies and community groups.

Ian's office is cluttered with reports, books with earnest-sounding titles about development and social justice, and piles of papers, while on his desk an army of paper clips have begun massing. The dreariness is lifted by a large, brightly coloured Latin American hunger cloth hanging on the wall. He is, I imagine, a man whose office is really in his head.

Knowing how to interpret the complex and rapidly changing world of international politics demands an agile mind. But here's a man who collects Ph.D.s – he has three, one honorary – like some people collect tea pots. He describes himself as a 'news junkie' and tries to keep up to date with the latest theological ideas about justice and development.

He is aware that we live in a Western society where patience has given way to a desire for instant solutions and answers. But as someone once remarked, every journey begins with a small step. And over the years, Ian – a man who sees a glass half full rather than half empty – and CIIR have taken many small steps.

'It's a mistake to ask development agencies what change did you bring about last week, because they'd probably say, 'None at all. Development is slow,' he insists. 'It's not a flash in the pan. You need enormous patience and have to face many setbacks before you see results.'

'We spend hardly any money on projecting ourself as an organisation and for that reason we're not well known in the Catholic community. We feel that's CAFOD's role. We're quite happy to take a back seat,' he says in his soothing, velvety voice.

Leafing though CIIR's 1997/98 annual review there are photos of Bolivian coca growers organising a roadblock in protest at government attempts to wipe out their crop; children in front of a bombed out building in Angola; veiled Yemenese women studying in a classroom; and Nicaraguans digging irritation ditches.

Despite his academic arsenal, Ian comes across as laid-back and unassuming as he talks about the achievements of CIIR with a quiet enthusiasm. For him, faith and politics are inseparable.

Born in Southall, west London, he and his older sister had a secure and happy childhood. 'Both my mother and father were extremely moral people; very, very strong moral convictions and very high standards of personal behaviour, though neither would have really claimed to be of any religious faith except sort of vaguely C of E, like a lot of people. And they were buried in an Anglican churchyard. My father was a very generous man after having had a very rough childhood in Hammersmith, which was then quite a poor area. His father died very young, leaving my grandmother destitute. She could barely sign her name. My father sold papers outside Hammersmith tube station to get enough money together for school.'

His father attained the rank of squadron leader during the Second World War and was the chief liaison officer for air-sea rescue between the British and Americans. Ian has only recently realised the important role his father played in the war and the lives he saved in the English Channel.

After the war, his family moved to Southend-on-Sea, Essex, where his father became a bank manager. 'I loved growing up in Southend because it meant I could go swimming every day. I love the mouth of the Thames area. I never feel completely happy unless I'm near the sea. It was much as it is now. It was a very popular fairly poor seaside resort. It was very much deck chairs, candy floss, dodgems, and people were doing summer jobs at the funfairs. East Enders would come for a day out. Very often the old rabbis would ask me why I wasn't in the synagogue.'

After leaving Southend-on-Sea High School for Boys, Ian went to St Catherine's College, Cambridge. In 1961 he went to work with the Emmaus community in what he says was 'the real backside of Paris, not the glossy image'. Set up by Abbé Pierre, a radical and visionary French priest, Emmaus introduced Ian to men and women who were living out a radical and dynamic Christianity.

He was particularly impressed by Fr Godefroi, a worker priest from Brittany. 'Although I was completely secular and had no religious convictions, I learned to respect and admire him while I was there, and I could see a man who was motivated by an intense concern for the poor.'

He worked with ex-members of the Foreign Legion, ex-convicts and 'ex this and ex that'. He worked as part of a gang who would clear out an apartment after someone had died, take it to a warehouse and then sell what was of any value to the rag-and-bone men. And working there a year later was an Englishwoman who was to become his wife.

He says he decided to become a Catholic more out of wanting to marry Jane, who came from a long line of Lancashire Catholics, rather than from any great awakening of faith. It wasn't until much later, while working in South Africa, that his political and religious beliefs really fused together.

'There wasn't any great conversion. I took instruction with Bill Yeomans of Southwell House in Hampstead. He was a fantastic Jesuit who later went off to the Far East where he worked with the refugee communities in Thailand. He came back, funnily enough, to die in London, in the hospice almost opposite where I am living at the moment in Stoke Newington. He and I got on very well together. He was a very pragmatic priest. I said, look I believe in all the stuff about Jesus but I don't believe in the blessed assumption, the immaculate conception and all this stuff about the Virgin Mary. And his line was that the important bit is about Jesus. So, in a way, I got received into the Church, according to the trade descriptions act, under false pretences. I remember going to confession in Soho Square and saying to the priest that I feel a bit worried that I don't believe in the blessed assumption. 'We Catholics, he said, da-da-da-da, as if *I* wasn't a Catholic!' His voice trails off into laughter. 'So this was how I first entered the Catholic Church. It was a kind of hole in the corner job.'

He was received into the Church in a quiet ceremony in a back room at Southwell House in 1963, far removed from the way people are received into the Church today, he notes with a tinge of envy. 'One of the lovely things about Catholicism is that it doesn't actually expect you to be converted on day one. It just expects you to make a little step. I think the Church is very sensible about this. So, it wasn't a very noble reason that brought me into the Church unless you consider marrying your wife a noble reason, which I do.'

After completing a Ph.D. in cell biology at Middlesex Hospital Medical School, he worked for a year lecturing at the University of Galway. Then, feeling a little like an Irish immigrant, he flew to the USA to take up a post at the Rockefeller University, New York. To his great surprise, Catholics whom he and his young family got to know in Manhattan provided both furniture and friendship to ease their transition.

'After we got married we joined the Teams of Our Lady. It was a French movement for married spirituality and very old-fashioned in many ways. The Teams of Our Lady in New York had bee told of our arrival. I saw what the Church could be. We were supported both spiritually and materially. It was a really live community.'

Ian soon bumped into the Catholic Worker Movement and what he calls the 'radical Catholic left'. When, in 1968, he was drafted for the Vietnam war he declared himself a conscientious objector, to the anger of the American authorities. 'If you were a pacifist or a Quaker they would accept this, but not if you were a Catholic. This meant that I was given a high status and was potentially on the next plane to Da Nang. So I decided I had better get out quick.' He did, and to Malawi in Africa, which was his introduction to the developing world.

You suspect that, stepping off the plane in Malawi, which had by then gained independence but had become under its president Dr Banda a one-party state, the twenty-seven-year-old Ian Linden was really fired up. Here too, his political beliefs soon got him into trouble. Dr Banda took exception to some of the things he heard this Englishman was teaching, not at the university, where he taught biology, but, worse, at the seminary. He was given a one-way ticket back to London. During his time in Malawi his mother discovered she had ovarian cancer. He says with gratitude in his voice that he was at her bedside when she died in 1973.

Ian then set about gaining another Ph.D., this time in African Studies at the School of Oriental and African Studies. Equipped with this, he returned to Africa in 1973 and taught the history of science and African history at Ahmadu Bello University, Nigeria. Here, his children had, he notes, the unusual experience of being the only white children in their school.

Getting out of his chair, he reaches for a large piece of card upon which are mounted photos of his time in Chad in 1980, explaining that Fr Pedro Adrupe commissioned him to compile a report on the refugee crisis in Africa.

He points to the card: 'There's the priest anointing the catechuemens in the open air. And there's one of the reasons they're outside.' His fingers rest on a pile of rubble that was once a Catholic cathedral. 'There's the presbytery,' he adds with a note of incredulity, moving his finger to a pick-up truck.

An extremely modest man, he allows himself a rare pat on the back and reveals that, as a consequence of his report, the Jesuit Refugee Service was born.

After a spell as a freelance writer and a spot of teaching

at Hamburg University he joined CIIR in 1980 and found himself working with Julian Filochowski, now his opposite number at CAFOD. For the next six years he came to grips with the injustices in South Africa, a period which was, he says, one of the most stimulating and formative in his life and where he really understood the political dimension to Christianity.

'I was largely colonised by black South Africans. After seven years of working with the radical Christians who were involved in the anti-apartheid struggle, I think I got a much deeper understanding of the importance for justice in Christianity, by watching them and learning from them.'

His frequent visits to South Africa introduced him to anti-apartheid activists such as Fr Albert Nolan and Dr Beyers Naude, men whose commitment and faith left a lasting impression on him. 'One of my happiest memories in South Africa was going each morning to Mass in Mayfair, one of the poorer areas of Johannesburg, and sitting around a simple table,' he recalls brightly, quipping that he was so close he almost consecrated the host himself. So where was he when Nelson Mandela was released from prison in 1990? 'I was in Trafalgar Square with a bottle of wine,' he chuckles.

Looking at Africa today, he becomes sombre and pessimistic and concedes that CIIR could do more to change the fortunes of this vast continent plagued by war, brutalities, poverty, corruption, Aids, a rickety infrastructure, debt, and a lack of Western investment.

'The real crisis in Africa is a crisis of political leadership. The political leadership in Africa is appalling. There are a whole variety of reasons for this. The major one is that the African nation state is very young. Secondly, the level of education of political leaders was on the whole very low because of the failure of colonial authorities to train a broad number of people adequately. I think in many ways it's a failure of vision, it's a failure of democracy. There's no way that these people are held to account by their citizens.'

So what difference does the Church make? 'In many African countries the only bit of the country that works is the Church. It's the only body where you have a proper postal service. It's the only thing where there's real development work going on, very often. The Church, almost like in the Middle Ages, in places like the Congo provides little centres of security and development – though, of course, in Rwanda it didn't.'

Ian concludes that if it wasn't for discovering liberation theology in the late 1970s when he first made connections with CIIR he probably wouldn't have remained a Catholic. Fr Gustavo Gutierrez's 1972 book *A Theology of Liberation* is credited with launching the liberation theology movement. 'For me, liberation theology was a very fundamental experience because here was theology that made sense of the world as I knew it. It was a spirituality that was really human and rooted in live experience. As far as I was concerned it gave Christianity a new sense of meaning and a new lease of life. Up until this time, a lot of the spirituality I had come across before this was very disincarnate. It was very much up in the air and didn't have much to say about your daily life.'

So how would he define liberation theology? 'The fundamental idea is that God's option is for the poor and therefore if you are going to be a Christian that has got to be your option too. Jesus comes to bring good news, not to the rich particularly – but it is for the rich if they can see it – but he comes with good news for the poor, those suffering from the yoke of opposition. And you could see plenty of that around in the 1970s and 1980s in Latin America and Africa.'

How, then, does liberation theology translate into life in modern Britain? He thinks for a moment and leans sideways on his chair. 'Well, I think with great difficulty. In all honesty, you would have to ask some of the British liberation theologians for their view. My own work since 1978 has really been on the problems of poverty and the oppression of a political kind in the poorest countries of the world. My work hasn't been on domestic poverty and – perhaps rather shamefully – what's going on down the road from me in Hackney or the slums of Glasgow or wherever.' He suggests that in parts of Britain where there is genuine poverty, and where people experience being on the underside of an affluent society, people understand liberation theology.

Both the USA and the Vatican were frightened of liberation theology, he claims, because of what was seen as its Marxist flavour. The Vatican, by not supporting the spread of liberation theology, is partly responsible for the weakening of the Catholic Church in Latin America, he strongly believes.

'A lot of the Latin American Church has fallen away. Out of the remains of it Californian churches and sects have hoovered up huge numbers of Catholics. Guatemala was once about 90% Catholic and now it's probably about 60% Catholic. It's pretty clear that the Vatican didn't put its weight behind the really living, flourishing movement that was liberation theology. It tried to block it. It was a big mistake but quite an understandable one. I don't see how a Polish pope could have possibly understood liberation theology. And it was just inevitable coming from that background that he would get the wrong end of the stick. And there were plenty of people to help him get the wrong end of the stick, in my opinion.'

In 2000 he made what turned out to be a somewhat perilous trip to the small African state of Burundi to help run peace workshops for the Justice and Peace commissions in seven different dioceses. With over 50,000 people killed in the civil war since the 1990s, Burundi is a dangerous place to visit. On his first night, he was advised to keep the lights off, avoid the windows, and get into the main passage of the house if attacked. When he turned up at the Jesuit Centre at Kirri to lead a workshop he found the bullet holes in the conference room 'a little off-putting'. Later, conversation was interrupted by the sounds of gunfire from the town below. When Ian remarked to the head of the Church's national reconciliation programme that he must get used to such things, he was told that you don't, but you have to master your fear.

He was deeply impressed by the way people risked their lives each day in their struggle for peace. 'It was an important moment for me because it was the first time I had ever done workshops on peace, bringing in the theology of reconciliation. It was very moving working with such courageous people who have such commitment.'

With so many governments and big businesses using sophisticated public relations methods to present a cuddly image to the world, CIIR's work in digging deep into policies to discover what is really buried there has earned it respect, and, you suspect, made it unpopular in some circles, not least amongst those slick professional lobbyists.

Despite, or maybe because of, its radical perspectives on international policy making, CIIR is regularly consulted by government departments, including the Foreign Office, the Department of Trade and Industry, and the Department for International Development.

'We're clear that even if we get money from a government department, that won't stop us criticising that department. We're consulted much more than we were under the Conservative government. It doesn't mean that the government acts, but at least we get a foot in the door.'

With the collapse of Communism in Eastern Europe and the ending of apartheid in South Africa, Ian suggests cautiously that the world in the nineties was less polarised and complicated than in the eighties. But as Kosovo, Rwanda, India, Iraq, and East Timor remind us, CIIR's vision of global peace and justice is still a long way off.

Telling me that during the nineties CIIR had become increasingly involved with multi-nationals over implementing ethical standards, he reaches for his briefcase and hands me a report entitled *Open Trading: Options for Effective Monitoring of Corporate Codes of Conduct*. Always grateful for bedtime reading, I thank him.

'More and more it's in the interest of big companies to present themselves as responsible moral agencies in the world because they're concerned about image and how the workforce feel about them. And people now feel that what people do in business is of moral concern.'

CIIR has pressed the oil company BP to review its social and ethical policies and it has also been instrumental in the drafting of European Union drugs legislation and in The Jubilee Campaign to abolish Third World debt.

Looking at the future, he grimaces and confesses he is troubled by the way the world's future is unfolding. 'Having grandchildren gives you a sense of the future and you want there to be justice and freedom. Praying for their future is very important; praying for that to come true. I'm quite worried about the future, in terms of the environment, in terms of the way things are going in society and so on. I'm horrified of leaving my grandchildren in a world which is suffering from terrible global warming, climate change, drought in Africa ... terrible changes. You see the future and obviously you're not in it. But you have this enormous responsibility to the people who are. It's all very well taking about social justice now but what about a bit down the road? What sort of world are we going to leave to these people? And what will they think when they look back on us? When they are living in a desert they will think, "They did that to us because they were so selfish and couldn't be bothered to alter the way they lived".'

His children are all high-flyers: one's a barrister, another a journalist, another a special adviser to a government minister, and the other works in film and animation. Not to be outdone, his wife is director of One World Action, which Ian describes as a mini-Oxfam, a charity started in 1991 by Glenys Kinnock. A lot of her work is trying to persuade actors, actresses and MPs to support various issues and projects. Instead of 'his' and 'hers' towels Ian and Jane probably have 'peace' and 'justice' written on theirs, I muse. When all the Lindens gather round the table at the family home in Stoke Newington, the conversation must resemble The Moral Maze.

As we closed the interview, I asked him what his idea of paradise is. Not Burundi, surely? Suffolk, he replied to my surprise. 'My idea of paradise is a swim off Southwold, fish and chips at Dunwich and a pint – or maybe more than one – of Adnams. And for a real treat, Cromer crab for tea,' he bubbles. A very English idea of paradise for such an international man.

The National Front Member

'Recently, I was standing on the platform at Mile End station when two Asian chaps came up to me and asked if I was Joe Pearce. Given my past, I thought to myself that I was going to be attacked. I took a step back and replied warily, yes. 'You don't remember me, do you?' asked one of them. I thought I had probably met him at some counter-demonstration or been involved in a fight with him, so I was expecting violence. Then he told me he'd been at school with me. The image of him came back to me. But the ironic thing was that he had become a militant Islamist. He began to sympathise with my National Front views, assuming that I was an anti-semite and would be against Israel. In order not to cause a scene I hummed and ha'd until he went on his way.'

Joseph Pearce laughs when he recounts this story, but it's not a belly-laugh. It's rather an uneasy laugh. For this encounter brought him to face with a dark period of his life; a period wen he was one of the leading exponents of a political creed of racial supremacy; a period of his life when, as he says, 'I had twisted myself into a grotesque gargoyle.' So seriously and passionately did he take his beliefs that, aside from demonstrations and violence, he stood as a National Front parliamentary candidate on three occasions and served two prison sentences for publishing material that was likely to incite racial hatred.

I had expected to be sitting with Joseph in his house in a town a few miles away deep in that vast, flat Norfolk countryside, not sitting on a settee in the coffee lounge of the eighteenth-century Duke's Head Hotel in King's Lynn Market Place. But the one and a half hour train journey from Kings Cross in London had turned into one of those epics that are only too common on the British railway system. The train had halted unexpectedly in the Cambridgeshire countryside and remained there for the next hour. The London-bound train on the next track had broken down. So, as a couple of hundred bemused and anxious passengers, along with their bicycles, buggies and baggage, were shepherded, like refugees, onto the King's Lynn train to return up the line to Ely in order – they hoped – to come back down the line to go on to London, I phoned Joseph to tell him about the delay and he generously offered to meet me in King's Lynn. Eventually I arrived at King's Lynn station, by coach, after the train, again unexpectedly, terminated at Downham Market. Joseph arrived about the same time, on a local bus.

A chunky man with a youthful face topped by short sandy hair, Joseph has lived in Norfolk since 1989 when he decided he'd had enough of London and that he also wanted to make a fresh start with his life. He now lives in a small house with his fifteen-year-old son from a marriage that was annulled. His seventeen-year-old daughter lives with his parents in Barking, east London. His time is spent researching his next book and writing at his PC in the living room. A self-confessed fitness fanatic, he tells me he regularly cycles, goes for long walks and does weight training.

Hearing his London accent you might conclude that, living in Norfolk, he was the proverbial fish out of water. Although he was born in Barking, in 1961, when he was eighteen months old his parents moved to Haverhill in Suffolk, attracted by the prospect of a council house with a garden and a more rural lifestyle. Joseph was baptised into the Church of England but, aside from family weddings, he never set foot in a church. His father was a carpenter and his mother worked as a cleaner and in factories. They stayed in Haverhill for ten years, Joseph was given a younger brother, and then homesickness set in and they returned to Barking.

'This was an important time of life,' he says fondly. 'I used to go walking in the countryside and play in the cornfields. I remember the culture shock when we returned to the East End. The children all appeared to be more sophisticated and grown up.'

In 1973 he watched images on TV of starving children in Biafra and felt anger against rich and greedy western governments. Three years later, he joined the National Front, lying that he was sixteen in order to gain admission.

'I was completely hooked. I believed the Nationalist viewpoint was the only one that was correct. I read everything I could, went leafleting once a week, went to monthly branch meetings, and travelled on coaches to demonstrations across the country. This took place on a blank page so by the time I was eighteen the only thing I had in my head was this ideology.'

The ideology of the National Front provided him with an intellectual framework and a way of understanding the world. He had left school with eight O levels, wanting only to commit his life to the National Front. He had been caned for carving the initials 'N.F.' into a school wall. His dedication, enthusiasm and sharp mind led to him being appointed editor of *Bulldog*, the National Front's youth magazine.

'When I was younger I had this image that being British was something to be proud of. I believed Britain should be a leading player in the world and when I saw its decline I began to ask why. By the time I was nineteen I had rejected the concept of the British empire. The only reason that black people were here was because of the empire. From being an imperialist I became an anti-imperialist. From being a right-wing reactionary I became

Social Nationalist. The whole thing was a melting pot of developing ideas.'

He says he doesn't blame his parents for the political beliefs he came to hold. 'In the climate that I grew up in, at home and beyond, racism was endemic in the East End in the 1970s. It's difficult to imagine now how the atmosphere was. A few years before, you had thousands of dockers marching through the streets in support of Enoch Powell. I suppose if someone has grown up in an area and they see it changing drastically in a short period of time, the uncertainty that this engenders leads to resentment and fear. On the Thames View council estate I lived on in Barking at one stage there were thirty paid-up members of the young National Front.'

He explains that in the late 1970s the image of the National Front changed from being almost respectable right-wing Tory to that of skinhead thuggery and football hooliganism. When National Front demonstrations began to be attacked by opponents, the temperature rose and National Front members responded in kind. They would set up ambushes at places such as Canning Town market, where their newspapers sellers had been attacked. Political meetings would end up in mass brawls, with chairs flying across the room and people running for cover.

'Because of the violence those who were, you might say, pillars of society quickly pulled out and those who were looking for a fight very quickly got involved. Although I had a reputation as a hard man I never enjoyed that aspect of it. It was always an occupational hazard, if you like. I look back on it now and it makes me shiver. In 1976 here was a lot of what was called "Paki-bashing" going on. One gang – who I never met – were supposed to go round in SS uniforms and shoot people with air pistols and crossbows. The Dagenham Axe Klan were another group. They called themselves Nazi hippies and would get drugged up on LSD and go out and attack people.'

Through the 1980s he lived in bedsits in south London, drank heavily in the pubs which provided meeting places for National Front members, and then eventually helped to set up a racist record label, White Noise, which promoted bands such as the skinhead group Skrewdriver. He received a number of convictions for public order offences and a number of scars as a result of fights with opponents from the Socialist Workers Party and various other Marxist groups. During this time he had what he says was 'a short, disastrous marriage', from which his two children were born.

In the 1982 general election he stood as the National Front candidate for Mitcham and Morden. In the same year he was sentenced to prison for six months for editing *Bulldog*. He had two more attempts at getting elected to parliament, at by-elections in Greenwich and in Barking & Dagenham. He also took on the editorship of *Nationalism Today*, which he describes as a more highbrow publication than *Bulldog*.

'I was uneasy with the pro-Hitler stance of some of the National Front's leadership, and indeed many of its members. Publicly, the National Front denied any sympathy with Hitler. Privately, however, the cognoscenti, with a nod and a wink, paid homage to the Third Reich. These closet Nazis referred to any hint of socio-economic radicalism within the Nationalist movement as "Strasserite", a term of abuse in Hitlerite circles because it refers to the purging of the left-wing Strasser brothers from the Nazi party in the early 1930s. Gregor Strasser, who had been Hitler's deputy, was murdered, probably on the orders of Goebbels, on the infamous "Night of the Long Knives" in 1934. Gregor's younger brother, Otto, resigned from the Nazi Party in 1930 and formed the secretive Black Front, an anti-Hitler organisation which rejected the Führer's racial theories and his reactionary stance on economic issues. Since I came from a working-class background, Otto Strasser's radicalism was attractive, not least because I had always been sensitive to Trotskyite claims that members of the NF were merely "the shock troops of Capitalism".'

Alongside his political education, a spiritual awakening was beginning to take place. He describes this as a David and Goliath struggle between religious faith and political ideology. In 1980, in search of a road between Communism and Capitalism, he was advised to study the distributist ideas of G. K. Chesterton and Hilaire Belloc, two of the major Catholic thinkers and writers of the twentieth century.

'This person suggested two books by Chesterton, *The Outline of Sanity* and *The Well and the Shallows*. I bought *The Well and the Shallows* for one essay in it, "Reflections on a Rotten Apple". But I started to read the other essays, which were Chesterton's defence of Catholicism. At that time I was a member of the Orange Order and had opposed the Pope's visit to England. I wasn't a Protestant. It was just a political statement about extreme Loyalism. When I began to read Chesterton it hit me like a thunderbolt. And I thought, "I can't fault any of this. I can't fault the logic, the picture of the world he's painting". In the middle of this, Jehovah's Witnesses knocked at the door. So I pretended I was a Catholic just as an intellectual exercise and for a bit of amusement. And I was amazed at how effective Chesterton's arguments were in countering the arguments of my visitor. The seeds were sown then and I became a lover of Chesterton: his style, his heart, the way he looked at things. And through Chesterton I began to read Belloc.'

So what attracted him to Chesterton? 'You have someone with a gymnastic mind. There was a joie de vivre about him. When I was first introduced to him I was amazed by the way he sliced through issues to make sense of them. The way he used words was like watching swordplay,' he replies enthusiastically.

Had he given much thought to God? He pauses for a moment. 'I think I probably wanted to believe in God. I was probably an agnostic rather than an atheist. For example, at home my family would play gospel music by Elvis and Jim Reeves and after a few beers I would sing along to them. They used to touch me. But this was on a psychological, emotional level. It never happened on an intellectual level. God wasn't that important to me. There were more important things in the world than God – which is obviously an absurd thing to say, but that's the way things were.'

In 1985 he was sentenced to prison again for editing *Bulldog*, serving six months of a twelve-month sentence, first in Wormwood Scrubs and then at Standford Hill on the Isle of Sheppey.

So how did prison affect him? 'I think prison was very important in my spiritual and emotional development. It taught me asceticism. The first time I went in I was militant and saw myself, like the IRA members, as a political prisoner. I did rigorous physical training. For the first few weeks in prison I was put in solitary confinement, which I loved. There was an NF campaign to get me out of it but I didn't want to get out,' he chuckles. 'I was locked up for twenty-three hours a day, but I was reading and writing. I wrote a political diatribe book, which was smuggled out.

'The second time was different. It was a devastating experience. Then, I was losing my political faith and groping towards a religious faith. This experience put me in touch with God. I remember somebody sending me rosary beads when I was in Wormwood Scrubs and for the first time in my life I tried to pray. I began to read *Apologetics and Catholic Doctrine* by Sheehan, which was an RE text book, and another on the works of St Thomas Aquinas. It all seemed to make so much sense. I began going to Mass in the prison chapel and when I came out I would have called myself a Catholic.' Nevertheless, he didn't break the links with the National Front immediately upon release. The organisation had been torn apart by a civil war and Joe, out of loyalty to his friends, tried to restore unity.

'It was awful because I wasn't really interested in the politics. I had really had enough and wanted to pull out. But because of the injustices my friends had suffered I stayed on. I stood for an election campaign in Greenwich but my heart wasn't in it. After about six months I finally left the NF. It all ended with a bad taste in the mouth. I had become disillusioned with the politics and felt betrayed by some of my friends.'

He started undergoing instruction with the rebel Society of St Pius X, but, because of what he says were 'difficulties' in his private life, decided not to continue. No doubt now he would say it was a blessing in disguise. After ten months working for a printing company in the City and living with his parents, he decided he had had enough of London and moved to Norwich in order to make a new start in life. He rented a bedsit in the city centre and landed a job at a book wholesalers. He began going to Mass at Our Lady Mother of God in Thorpe, eventually recommenced instruction and then on St Joseph's day in 1989 was received into the Church.

As an act of thanksgiving to both God and Chesterton, he decided in 1991 to write a Chesterton biography, feeling that none of the previous works had painted a full and accurate picture of the man. For four years he worked on the book during every spare moment he had. His manuscript was accepted, he received half of an advance and resolved to try and make a career as a writer, something he had always found fulfilling. Looking back, he admits it was a superhuman effort, but a gamble that – 'through providence or whatever' – has paid off.

After this he wrote a novel within six weeks – 'it was all there in my head' – found a small Catholic publisher and then straightaway began work on *Literary Converts*, an exploration of the spiritual lives of Ronald Knox, Evelyn Waugh, J. R. R. Tolkien, T. S. Eliot, Graham Green and other great writers of the twentieth century. A quote from Evelyn Waugh sets the scene for the book: 'Conversion is like stepping across the chimney piece out of a looking-glass world, where everything is an absurd caricature, into the real world God made; and then begins the delicious process of exploring it limitlessly.'

In order to research the book, Joseph travelled to meet relatives and friends of many of the writers and also spent large chunks of time at a desk in the University of East Anglia library. Weaving all the various strands together was difficult compared to writing about one person, he concedes.

'The thing which was most intriguing about *Literary Converts* was that it revealed a network of minds and a network of grace. Writers from different backgrounds, different outlooks and writing different types of books. If you look at, say, Oscar Wilde, Alexander Solzhenitsyn and J. R. R. Tolkien and look at what they wrote you couldn't get further away from each other if you tried. You have the flippant almost cynical society farces of Wilde, the ultra-serious, deeply political and philosophical sagas of Solzhenitsyn and the almost escapist fantasy of Tolkien. If you see them in isolation they are eons apart. But in fact in these writers you see a sense of suffering, metaphysical exile, the idea that we are not really in our true home here and are divorced from where we are really meant to be. And if you look at *The Picture of Dorian Gray, Cancer Ward* or *Lord of the Rings* they address issues of carrying crosses and these crosses becoming lighter once you allow grace to work. So whereas the literary form may be drastically different you have certain key motifs, which are essentially spiritual and address Man's relationship with his creator and that of the universal with himself.'

When I ask him for his verdict on Graham Greene, he responds flatly that he finds Greene's description of himself as an agnostic Catholic unconvincing. He believes the two terms are contradictory. He points out that, like Greene, Malcolm Muggeridge had led a rather dissolute life and had had a string of extra-martital affairs. However, Muggeridge's soul had been touched and his life changed by an encounter in Calcutta with Mother Teresa when he was filming a BBC TV documentary. By contrast, when Greene attended a Mass in southern Italy celebrated by the mystic Blessed Padre Pio, no inner conversion was set in motion, seemingly at least, although it is said that he carried a photo of Padre Pio in his wallet until the day he died.

Much modern literature is amoral relativism which is devoid of any depth, claims Joseph. 'These books are a bit like the literary form of TV's *Eastenders*. Everyone is terribly obnoxious and thoroughly miserable. No one ever has any joy, true contentment or transcendent spirituality. It's all about people staggering blindly from one selfish knee-jerk reaction to the next, making everyone's life miserable including their own. I cannot really see how this lowest common denominator shallowness can be sustained. I believe people will want something with more substance, that is more challenging and more questioning and that addresses issues of good and evil, spirituality, God's existence.'

He now has an impressive body of work under his belt, including biographies of J. R. R. Tolkien and Solzhenitsyn. He is currently writing a biography of Belloc and another of South African born poet and Catholic convert Roy Campbell, who, Joseph claims confidently, was one of the greatest poets of the twentieth century, but has been largely written out of the literary canon, partly because he fought for Franco in the Spanish Civil War. Joseph says his mission is to introduce some of the great Christian thinkers to a wider audience.

Returning to the theme of political beliefs, Joseph argues that Catholic social teaching transcends political parties, though many Catholics, even teachers in Catholic schools, are largely ignorant of it. 'The Social teaching of the Church is not materialistic. It doesn't believe in the market as a means of measuring success. Nor does it believe that the state has a right to interfere in the sovereign rights of families. It can't be called Socialist or Communist, nor can it be called Capitalist. It's the truth and it transcends left and right. The writer and friend of C. S. Lewis, Christopher Derrick, called the left-wing divide the "damn fool dichotomy". When you get these left/right divisions it's because people haven't digested the social teaching of the Church and they are often looking at politics or economics through a secular prism.'

Despite the marginalisation of Catholicism in modern secular Britain and the decline in the practice of the faith, he says, with boldness in his voice, that he is not pessimistic about the future of the Church. Far from it. 'If you look at the history of the Church over the last 2000 years there have been major crises in every decade, major scandals, major issues of members of the Church getting it wrong and society being barbaric. Five hundred years ago the Reformation would have been seen as the end, and before that some might have thought the same in the Dark Ages. Yet the Church has always emerged as the voice of sanity. The fact that those of us today who are trying to be saints are in a minority shouldn't surprise us. Events of the world are transient and pass. Truth is eternal.'

The Scientist

On route to her doctorate in biochemistry, Josie Callaghan was invited to apply for what she calls a 'plum job' in Denmark. But the anti-God ethos of the scientific culture had started to make her feel uncomfortable. Then, after a serious car accident, she found herself rethinking not only her career goals but how she lived out the Catholic faith she had been brought up in.

Wearing a green turtleneck sweater and baggy grey trousers, Josie looks like your average bubbly, single thirty-something. Seeing her in the supermarket you might conclude she was just preoccupied with finding 'Mr Right', planning her next career move and booking that holiday for a fortnight's sun and sea.

Instead, she is now living as a member of a young Catholic lay community in a house in Leeds. Her days are no longer spent peering through a microscope but in prayer and with the Youth 2000 team planning and giving retreats in Catholic schools. Yet a few years ago, Josie was, she admits, an average Catholic. Her faith, like many cradle Catholics, had grown very little as an adult.

One of six children, her Irish father left home when she was young, leaving her Nigerian mother to cope alone in Catford, south-east London. 'We didn't miss our dad,' she says firmly. 'I didn't find it a problem being brought up by my mum. She was a strong woman; a typical Nigerian.'

Her mother provided her and her brothers and sisters

with a rock solid spiritual foundation, she says with admiration. 'Your first priority was your faith. You went to Mass come rain, come shine. It was religion, family, education. I didn't think about my faith. It was just there. I never went through the rebellious stage, like some teenagers. So I accepted my faith at face value. I believed in God because my mother told me to. This didn't mean I didn't have a relationship with God when I was young. I felt close to God and I used to talk to the holy pictures in our house all the time. I remember during my O levels I took all my holy pictures into the exams and arranged them on my desk. When I couldn't understand a question I gave them meaningful looks. Needless to say, I got some very strange looks from the other pupils and teachers.'

Her commitment to her school work paid off and in 1988 she was accepted by the University of London's Queen Mary and Westfield College to study a degree in biochemistry and organic chemistry. 'When I began university I still considered myself a good Catholic, but my religion became a routine. Although I believe in the Catholic faith, I didn't live it in my heart. I was a stereotypical one-hour-a-week Catholic, going into church on a Sunday and then coming out to continue living my life the way I wanted,' she recalls.

She enjoyed delving further into the world of science and, after graduating, opted to begin the long haul towards a Ph.D., at the University of Southampton. 'During this time I really lost my relationship with God. I knew He was still there but I stopped talking to Him and any prayers I said were usually rushed and out of guilt. I said them because I had always said them – and also because I didn't want to spend a long time in purgatory! I tried to convince myself I was happy, but I wasn't. I enjoyed myself but there was an emptiness in what I was doing. I felt I had lost something.

'None of my friends or colleagues believed in any faith. They were either agnostic or simply against organised religions. When we went to the pub the argument was always about the Church getting rich from church collections, not helping the poor enough. They all advocated free sex, artificial contraception and a woman's right to choose an abortion. They believed people who were religious were like sheep. Even then, I could never agree with this. Although I didn't have a good knowledge about my faith I always felt deep down that the Church had the truth, except on the issue of artificial contraception. I didn't understand the Church's position and was openly against it.'

Her studies were going well until, driving through Winchester one day, her car spun out of control and ploughed into a tree. She sustained broken ankles and knees, ribs and skull and spent the next thirteen weeks in hospital. 'I can't actually point to the time where my faith began to deepen. But it must have been around this time. God gave me the grace to be in hospital,' she says reflectively. 'Before the accident I'd applied for a job at the Carlsberg brewery in Copenhagen. And, as I knew the person who had spoken to me about the post, I felt I had a very good chance of getting it.'

For someone who is a keen keen hiker, horse-rider and cyclist, being cooped up in hospital for so long was not easy. 'I had a video and TV and family and friends would come round,' she says, then, rippling into laughter, adds, 'When I was given a wheelchair my friends used to take me down to the pub!'

After leaving hospital she spent a year at home convalescing. 'I really began to think more about my faith and use my mind as well as my heart,' she says. She went with her family to a retreat house in County Tyrone, Ireland, run by 'the two Patricks', two men who claim to receive messages from Jesus. It turned out to be a pivotal moment in her life.

'I loved God. I loved Jesus and I loved Our Lady. But during this time, Jesus came down off the altar and became a friend I could really talk to. Sitting in the prayer room in the attic, I began to see Jesus as someone real.'

Resuming work on her Ph.D., she found she was beginning to look at the world of science in a different way. And by now she was working as a volunteer amongst the homeless in central London. 'I just wanted to leave that world of science. I knew it wasn't for me. It was dragging me down,' she says, shaking her head to emphasise the point. 'My supervisors couldn't believe why I'd gone to the retreat house. And many of my friends now think I'm wasting myself.'

Relations between science and religion, once two sides of the same coin, have become fractured during the explosion of knowledge in the last 400 years. In the euphoria of rapid technological progress in the nineteenth century the German philosopher Friedrich Nietzsche famously declared, 'God is dead'. Theories of relativity, the Big Bang, cloning, 'Frankenstein foods' and knowledge of the human genes, amongst other things, have all served to push God even further out of the cosmic picture.

Yet despite the huge scientific advances, often presented in terms of unlocking the secrets of the universe, it is only religion which claims to offer an answer to the 'why' rather than the 'how' questions of life. Science can only analyse and dissect the natural, not the supernatural. At the heart of Christianity, with its belief in the hidden God of creation, incarnation, resurrection and redemption lies faith and mystery.

Josie sees no contradiction between science and faith, arguing that the reason so many highly intelligent scientists reject God is because they have bought into negative media images of religion and also, perhaps, given in to pride.

'To survive in the scientific world, you have to keep your religion separate from your work. The whole concept of science to me is a hypothesis you have to test out. Yet the media often present these theories as if they were facts.'

I suggest that the modern world may have found technology but lost its soul. She nods vigorously in agreement and adds confidently, 'The more I know about science, the more I know about the body, the more I know about enzymes, it increases my wonder and faith in God. This is proof for me, if proof were needed.'

So how does she view the Biblical account of creation? She thinks for a moment. 'On the one hand the evidence is there for evolution. But on the other hand there are many missing links. I take the Old Testament stories from Abraham onwards as, generally, factual. But the stores in Genesis of Adam and Eve, the Tower of Babel and Noah and the flood I see as literary devices for explaining deep truths about who are and who God is.'

Josie was invited by some friends to spend a week at Abbaye Blanche in Mortain, Normandy, France, one of over thirty houses in France run by the dynamic Community of the Beatitudes. 'I'd never heard of them before and I thought it was a great opportunity to have a cheap holiday. I remember saying to one of my friends that the community was beautiful but the structured way of praying was too rigid for me. I needed my own space and independence. But by the end of the week my view had changed and I felt a deep peace and began to find community life attractive. But the idea of living that kind of life was scary. I returned to the abbey and spent a month there. This time God opened my eyes to see how right this way of life was for me. The spirituality of the community was what I had been seeking for years without even knowing it. I knew then that I was being called into a community way of living.'

The spirit amongst the priests, nuns and lay people who have decided to live together at Abbaye Blanche has greatly impressed her. 'They're really interested in the roots of faith. The community celebrates the Shabbat and many of the Hebrew festivals. It's drawing out the Jewishness of Christianity. I'd never thought of Our Lady or St Peter as Jewish!'

She adds that she finds it easy to pray but is now learning to read the Bible in a more prayerful way. 'When Jesus talks to the people in first-century Palestine I now know that he is also talking to me personally. Although I never went away from my faith,' she muses, 'I wasn't living a truly Catholic life. It was only through an opening up of Jesus' humanity and loving him as a friend that I began to realise that when I did wrong, I was hurting a friend and causing him pain.'

Candidly, she admits to being uncertain about where specifically her vocation lies. Her doctorate is, she knows, a passport to a lucrative career, should she ever embark on a career as a scientist. However, if her year in Leeds goes well, she will join the Community of the Beatitudes in France. It all depends on to where she feels God is calling her, she says.

'God is giving me the opportunity I have hungered for, the opportunity to stand up and witness to his love. It's very tiring but when I go to bed at night I feel fulfilled. It's funny how my life has changed so much from a couple of years ago, especially in the things I want. I thought I would be happy with the faith I had, a car, and a bank balance that allowed me to take at least three holidays a year. I no longer have the car and the bank balance, but I am truly happy and at peace in my life, which is centred around regular prayer and daily adoration. If somebody had told me a couple of years ago that I would have no career and be living in a community I would have laughed my head off and wondered if they needed to be institutionalised. God is good.'

The Politician

'Ann's had to go and vote,' I am told apologetically by a researcher when I reach Ann Widdecombe's office in one of those anonymous buildings in Whitehall.

I am directed into Miss Widdecombe's inner sanctum, and, by way of compensation, placated with a cup of full-flavoured coffee, and left to my own devices. Surprisingly, it's quite small. At one end is the great lady's desk, replete with an 'in, read, out, tray'. At the other, a table and chairs. Miss Widdecombe, as you might expect, has added her personal touch to alleviate the bureaucratic drabness. A poster with a pink hippopotamus and a cat has the caption: 'If you want to look thinner hang around people fatter than you.' Several anti-abortion posters occupy a large notice board; a rosary dangles from the wall, which also displays a number of photos of family and friends; a pile of *House of Lords Official Reports* are stacked on a chair; and a large toy black cat decked with blue 'Win With Widdecombe' badges sits on a shelf. I spy *The Power of Positive Prayer* sandwiched between less spiritual works.

Eventually, Miss Widdecombe, MP for Maidstone and The Weald and Shadow Home Secretary, swoops into the office in a military right-let's-get-down-to-it manner and taxis down on a chair opposite me. She's wearing a blue dress, yellow blouse underneath (not quite the Papal colours, I muse) and has a silver cross around her neck. Her hair is jet black and styled in the manner of the

Beatles, although – just in case you're wondering – there's no sign of a guitar. A pearl necklace, ear rings and a gold bracelet add a hint of glamour.

It was in 1993 that Miss Widdecombe became a Catholic, or, as some might put it, a Seedling. Sitting down opposite me, she says matter-of-factly that she feels as if she's been a Catholic all her life. 'It was undeniably the best decision I ever took,' she adds briskly. 'It wasn't easy at the time. But I did the right thing.'

What forced her, and many others, including several hundred clergy, to jump ship was the decision in 1992 by the General Synod of the Church of England to permit women to the priesthood. As time doesn't permit her to go over her story she refers me to *The Path to Rome*, where it is set out in the kind of incisive, robust style we have come to expect from Miss Widdecombe.

She wrote: 'On the evening the Synod decision was announced I left the Church into which I had been baptised and confirmed and in which I had (save for a period of agnosticism) always practised my Christianity. But I did not know where I was going. Many people assumed I opted for Rome at once, but in fact it was only four months later that I finally made that decision. The reality was that I was not doctrinally at one with Rome, that I found some of its practices hopelessly superstitious and that I was not a high Anglican with one foot already over the Tiber.

'I had admired the Roman Catholic Church from afar for a long time as it seemed to stand alone in being ready to promulgate teaching which was at odds with the permissive weave of society in general. Rome stood for Christian morality with no regard to what might or might not be fashionable or popular or easy to achieve. The Pope's encyclical *Veritas Splendor* had not then been published, but its sentiments had been the guiding light of the Catholic Church for nearly two millenia.

'One can admire without necessarily agreeing and that was my attitude to Rome. I hated Marian doctrine, dismissed purgatory, was repulsed by the sacrificial nature of the Mass, laughed at indulgences. Oddly the concept of papal infallibility gave me no trouble at all. Jesus had clearly said to Peter, "Whatsoever thou shalt bind on earth shall be bound in Heaven. Thou art Peter and upon this rock I will build my Church." Similarly, the Real Presence of Christ's body and blood gave me less cause for doubt than it might have done for many Anglicans.'

She sought out Fr Michael Seed, Cardinal Hume's ecumenical adviser, whom she had met at the launch of his first book a couple of years earlier. She began a long series of conversations that resolved many but not all of her doubts. These doubts were finally resolved when she met with Cardinal Hume, an encounter which made her feel she had a tangible link with the Early Church.

Predictably, her reception into the Church resulted in a media circus. What was less predictable was the thousands of letters she went on to receive. Some welcomed her; others castigated her; others said the Church of England was glad to be rid of her.

The determining factor in her decision to leave the Church she had grown up in and learnt to love was the question of authority. She concluded that the Bible alone cannot provide the authority necessary in living the Christian life. It needs to be interpreted. And only the Catholic Church can claim the apostolic descent that gives it the authority to pronounce on doctrine and morality.

'Many other Christians have difficulty with the exclusive nature of the Church; its interdict on inter-communion, its insistence that it alone possesses the fullness of truth. This, however, is a reflection of our times when it is unfashionable to be sure of anything, when anything is tolerated except intolerance and when every individual is infallible except the Pope. It can not be a serious objection though it is one which is often put forward.'

So what of her Anglican upbringing? 'The Anglican experience was part of my Christian journey. It would be silly to think that my spiritual journey began when I was received into Rome.' She tells me that her confirmation name is Hugh after the Protestant martyr Hugh Latymer. Her brother is an Anglican canon in Bristol.

Fr Michael Seed had told me that Miss Widdecombe dislikes the smell of alcohol on the breath. It is true, I ask, gingerly? A pained good-Lord-no look appears across her face, and she tells me matter of factly that she and Fr Michael often open a bottle of whisky if they meet after Mass. Assuming that it is after Mass and not before, I press on with the questions, feeling like a schoolboy bowling to Brian Lara in the nets.

There are many words you could choose to describe Miss Widdecombe: capable, uncompromising, ultra-confident, pompous, vociferous, highly-motivated, authoritative, bristling, abrasive, energetic, tough, solid. And there are many jobs you could image her doing had she not entered parliament: headmistress, barrister, doctors' receptionist, army officer, librarian.

But sitting across the table from her, watching her deal snappily with each question, my mind drifted to Roger Hargreaves's *Mister* and *Miss* children's books. If Miss Widdecombe had a nickname at school, I mused, it could only have been Miss Bossy Boots.

But Miss Bossy Boots does have a rather endearing quality to her, and, perhaps, a certain, if rarely glimpsed, vulnerability. For a woman who has chosen to marry politics rather than Mr Right (well, it's unlikely she'd marry Mr Left), there must be – surely? – moments of loneliness, longing and regret. But she has never publicly said so. My hunch is if she allowed a man into her life she would feel she had committed adultery. She says she enjoys her own company and the last thing she would want when she goes home is to find a husband waiting for her.

The conversation moves to prayer. Living such a hectic life, how does she fit it in? 'I pray as I go along. I only manage formal prayer a couple of times a week.' She paused for a moment and then adds with finality, 'It seems to work.'

There is today a heightened cynicism about politicians. As the former Russian leader Nikita Khrushchev once remarked, 'Politicians are the same all over. They promise to build a bridge even when there is no river.'

Her peripatetic childhood – 'a big chunk of it spent in Singapore' – her studies at the universities of Birmingham and Oxford, her time with Unilever and her twelve years as a senior administrator at the University of London, were all, she concludes, preparation for a career in politics.

'I didn't do much serious academic work at Oxford,' she admits, 'but enough to pass exams. I was pursuing other things: the Oxford Union, the Conservative Association. I did a lot of political reading rather than concentrate on a degree.'

Her job at the University of London provided her with a good deal of annual leave, which she used to kick off her political career, first in local government at Runnymeade and then at Burnley in 1979, where she failed to get elected as MP.

But when she did eventually get into parliament she soon began to make her mark, going into battle like an armoured car, locating her targets and then ... bang! As Thatcher and Major both eventually fell by the wayside Miss Widdecombe stuck at it and ended up as a government minister until Labour ended eighteen years of Tory rule in 1997.

Her father, a senior civil servant, must, surely, have influenced her in some way, although she cites her mother and the late Cardinal Basil Hume as the two key influences on her life. Her mother, now eighty-nine, lives with her in her Westminster flat.

So how does she handle the workload? 'You have to be organised. Most of the day does not consist of getting on with reading or signing. It consists of meeting after meeting, or interview after interview. It's only when this is all finished that you can get on with the desk work.'

Despite what she describes as a horrendous working week, consisting of meetings, lunches, dinners, dealing with policy decisions and signing hundreds of letters, she claims she couldn't think of doing anything else.

'I love the work. I have great confidence in what I'm trying to do. I wouldn't willingly do anything else.' What's the attraction of politics? 'I think that the biggest attraction of being in politics is trying to solve insoluble problems, either on the micro level or macro level.'

She has been unstinting, clear-sighted and eloquent in her defence of the unborn, and is more of a spear than a thorn in the side of the so-called feminists. They know they're up against it when Miss Bossy Boots ventures into the fray.

How does she deal with power and influence? 'Not difficult,' she replies curtly with a shake of the head that says next question. Has she seen any films recently? '*Life is Beautiful*. Wonderful.' Do you go often? 'Before *Life is Beautiful* I probably hadn't seen another film since *101 Dalmations*. I may be wrong ...'

Wobbling slightly, I ask if she does crosswords (don't ask me why). 'No. Latin translations, yes. Crosswords, no.' Well, that's the end of that one. What about TV, then? 'I don't possess a TV,' she replies combatively.

Her social justice commitment was questioned by some Catholics in 1994 when she dismissed the Archbishop of Canterbury's Easter sermon as a 'party political broadcast' because he had condemned the gap between the rich and the poor.

In 1999, CAFOD persuaded her to visit Zambia in the hope that they could persuade her to put her weight behind the campaign to write off Third World debt. 'I had made it abundantly clear – from start to finish – that I didn't expect my views to change,' she blusters, then, turning her guns on a newspaper report that said she had done a U-turn, she throws back her head and exclaims, 'Nonsense. Most awful nonsense. Nonsense.' She adds that she had been to Africa on previous occasions and didn't see anything that surprised her but, nevertheless, was still shocked by some of the poverty she witnessed.

'We have to solve the issues with the head as well as the heart. The people kept saying, "Make sure it comes to us not to the government." I was in tune with them, despite all the people at CAFOD doing the hand-wringing.' She then reveals that she is trying to raise money to support a school in Zambia.

With the publication of *The Clematis Tree*, she has now launched herself as a novelist. The book deals with, amongst other things, what happens to a middle-class family when their son suffers brain damage in a car accident. A central character is Sally, an MP who introduces a euthanasia bill and is then pursued by the media.

Reviews were, by and large, very favourable, although fellow politician turned novelist Edwina Currie rubbished it. 'One surprise is that the unmarried, childless author deals so sympathetically with family life, with jokes and pets,' commented Valerie Grove in *The Times*. Her next novel will be about a convent girl who falls in love with a married Nazi officer.

Having run dry of questions and aware that Miss Widdecombe is anxious to get cracking with BBC Radio who have arrived down in reception. I thank her – feeling a bit like the Invisible Man – and clumsily back out of the office. Had I been wearing a cap, I probably would have doffed it. The late Lord Hailsham once remarked that the moment politics because dull democracy is in danger. Well, one thing you can't say about Miss Widdecombe is that she's dull. That would be nonsense. Absolute nonsense.

The Gangster

One night in 1992, while working on the door of a night club in London's West End, John Pridmore ejected a man who was drunk. Angry, the man returned later with some friends and John found himself caught up in a fight as he and his colleagues struggled to get the men out of the club. In the melee, he struck the man, hard. A week later the police raided the night club and John was arrested and charged with grievous bodily harm. The man, it turned out, was in a critical condition in hospital. Fortunately, the man pulled through and a lack of evidence prevented a prosecution being brought against John. But, he recalls, coming so close to killing a man pulled him up sharp.

'This incident was a turning point in my life,' he says, shaking his head and lighting a Benson & Hedges. 'I knew something was seriously wrong. I didn't like what I had become, but I didn't know any other way. I came in touch with how unhappy I really was. I felt a great sense of emptiness. I had become very good at deceiving myself. I was looked upon as being one of the hard men of London and the reality was that I was scared. The more scared you are, the more violent you become. One one level, I had it all: a BMW, a Mercedes, the designer clothes and so much money that I could gamble £1000 in an afternoon and think nothing of it. As soon as I had money I would throw it away because I knew there were plenty of ways I could get more.'

There is a certain romance about the gangster. James Cagney, Robert De Niro, and Al Pacino have all made their mark on the big screen portraying men driven by power, reputation and money; men for whom violence was the way to achieve their objectives. In Britain, real life gangsters such as the Krays have become part of popular folklore and mythology. But behind the snazzy suit, the sleeked-back hair, the flashy cars and the wads of money can be an emptiness, as John discovered.

Sitting in a pub in Stratford, east London, thirty-five-year-old John, a burly, bearded, six-footer, tells me about how God dramatically broke through into his life one night and turned it upside down. The scattering of afternoon drinkers occasionally cast curious glances in our direction as, in between the pop music from the juke box, snippets of our conversation float across the pub.

His childhood had been spent up the road in Walthamstow. When he was ten his parents divorced and he went to live with his father, a policeman. The trauma of the divorce triggered his slide into crime. He began stealing and carrying out break-ins and at the age of fifteen he was sentence to a detention centre. Upon release, he got a job in a radio shop, but was soon stealing from the till. A motorcycle accident resulted in several months in hospital. During which time, he met a Catholic priest. It was an insignificant encounter, but one that stuck in his mind, and years later John went in search of this priest. At nineteen he was convicted of burglary and sent to a youth prison in Suffolk, where, locked up for twenty-three hours a day, he felt self-hate, anger and, at one point, contemplated suicide.

Returning to east London after his six months in prison, he was determined to do something with his life – and make some serious money. 'When I came out of prison I drifted back into petty crime and then I started to do some work for a well known East End villain who ran a second-hand shop. One day in the pub, his son offered me the chance to provide backstage security at places such as

Wembly Stadium and the Royal Albert Hall. I worked at all sorts of events, ranging from Queen and Simply Red concerts to Amnesty International events and boxing. It didn't pay that well, but it was a way into the more lucrative security world. After a year I moved into bouncing in West End night clubs, attracted by the big money that was an offer. I began to get into heavier crime and mix with some real villains. I was dealing in dope, cocaine, ecstasy and sulphate. I also got involved in forging MOTs and tax discs. I discovered that there really is an underworld that exists with its own rules, territories and ways of doing things, which usually involve violence.'

John moved in a seedy, neon-lit world of pubs, clubs and clandestine meetings in back rooms. Money was never in short supply and neither were women, attracted by the hard man image. Violence was simply part of the job. John provided the muscle when someone didn't pay up, when disagreements broke out between rival gangs or firms, or when the order went out to smash up a pub with a baseball bat. Having learnt tai jitsu, a martial art that combines karate, judo and boxing, he could handle himself. And if that didn't work the ammonia and machete he always carried would. The vicious revenge beating he gave to one man while he was picking up his son from school was, like much of the violence he engaged in, to protect and build up his reputation. But it was that fight at the night club that brought his life into sharp focus.

Soon after, sitting alone in his flat one night, he became aware of what he describes as a voice within. 'The voice told me about the really bad things I'd done. I felt in total darkness. I cried and prayed for another chance. It was an incredible experience. I knew God was real. As I walked out of the flat I said to God, "Up to now all I've ever done is take from you, now I want to give something back." As I said that prayer, for the first time in my life I felt the Holy Spirit and a great sense of forgiveness and peace. I went straight to my mum. When I told her about my experience she replied that she had been praying for me every day of her life. As a baby I had been baptised a Catholic but religion had never featured very strongly in my upbringing. My father, who was Church of England, didn't want us to have anything to do with the Catholic Church.'

At his mum's suggestion, he went to talk to the local parish priest, who recommended he went on a retreat at Aylesford Priory in Kent. A meeting there with a former heroin addict, who had lost his wife, children and home because of his addiction, and was now a social worker had a profound effect on John, who was still smoking dope. 'He told me about his life and how he'd ended up in a squat with absolutely nothing. Then,' he chuckles, 'he had an experience of God – on the toilet of all things. "Now I have God in my life," he said, "I don't need drugs".'

Cutting away from his colleagues, giving up the drugs and the bundles of tenners, and taming his aggression was not easy, he admits, despite this road to Damascus experience. 'Someone offered me £10,000 for my black book with all my contacts in it after I found God,' he reveals, 'but I burned it.'

A priest suggested he went to confession. 'At Westminster Cathedral I went to confession for the first time in my life and I experienced a real peace. It was probably the first time I switched off and didn't have to think about who I had to throw out or what drug deals I had to do,' he says.

John emerged from Westminster Cathedral feeling forgiven by God. The only prayer he knew was the Our Father. But, he explains, it took him much longer to forgive himself. Impressed by his testimony, his local Catholic priest encouraged him to undertake voluntary work with the youth club. He also began working at a drop-in centre for older people, and as a driver/carer.

He had invited him to attend a retreat being run by Youth 2000, an international organisation set up to evangelise young Catholics. But, he grins, on the day he was due to go some unexpected visitors turned up at his flat. 'Suddenly there was a knock at the door and nine Old Bill came pouring in and arrested me. I owed £2,700 in fines. They took me to Leyton nick and locked me in a cell. The next day I was standing in the dock at Walthamstow Magistrates' Court. I remember this screw who knew me really well saying, "You've got a really bad one today, John. She's in no mood for anything; she's got the right hump." When I saw her, I knew what he meant. "Mr Pridmore," she began, "we can see that you owe £2,700 in fines. How are you going to pay?" Before I could answer she added sarcastically, "We can see how it has played on your conscience because in the last ten years you have paid £7." When she sentenced me to prison for twenty days I protested that I was going on a retreat. "No you're not," she retorted, "you're going to Pentonville". I replied that I had found God, was doing voluntary work and could only pay £1 per week. She was unimpressed and said that the court was not going to wait 2700 days for me to clear my fine.'

A couple of months later, he did make it to a Youth 2000 retreat, at Aylesford, and it was a pivotal moment in his journey. 'The first talk I heard was by Fr Slavko. It was called "Give God your wounded heart". I remember looking at this cross as he gave the talk and for the first time in my life realising that Jesus loved me so much that he had gone through agony for me. I said to the Lord, "What is it you want me to do for you?" And I heard the words: "Go to confession". So I did and when the priest put his hand on my head I knew it was the hand of Jesus and I knew that he truly forgave me.'

Fasts and walking through the streets of the East End barefoot were some of the penances he undertook to atone for his sins; for the lives that he damaged.

He asked his parish priest in Leyton if he could give his testimony. 'All these people had seen me going to Mass and praying the rosary and they all probably thought, "What a lovely, holy young man". I just wanted them to know what I had been. Fr Hall said I could give my testimony when the kids met for a confirmation class. I was only expecting a few of them, but when I arrived there were about ninety kids, their sponsors and their families. There must have been about 350 people in the church! I was petrified as I stood up and began to tell them about my life. As I walked off the sanctuary a woman came up to me crying. It was amazing.'

His voluntary work not only provided a new lease of life for his energies but also gave him a sense of purpose. He landed a job as a youth advocacy worker with Hackney Social Services and spent two eventful years working with youngsters on the notorious Kingsmead Estate.

The job provided a stern test for his new found faith. Many of those attending the two youth clubs he helped to run came from the kind of family backgrounds most people only read about in those magazine articles about under-class Britain. Here, drugs, prostitution, violence, abuse, poverty and hopelessness were a reality.

He recalls an encounter one day with a teenager who had a reputation as a local tough guy. 'I challenged him after he had dented my car one day. He was egging me on to hit him. I grabbed hold of him and told him I should give him a good hiding. This is what he was expecting. But then I said, "I'm not going to do that – because I love you".'

Feeling the call to religious life and attracted by the spirit of St Francis of Assisi, he joined the Franciscan Friars of the Renewal in The Bronx, New York. The fiars sleep on the floor, rise each day at 5 a.m., spend long periods in prayer, and provide food and shelter for the poor. But after several months John felt that his vocation lay in Britain with inner-city kids.

He is now a youth worker in a Catholic parish in inner city Liverpool and a regional organiser for Youth 2000. He's paid just £50 per week and spends much of his time giving retreats in Catholic schools, where he shares his conversation story.

Given the romance and glamour – the Robert De Niro image – associated with being a gangster, teenagers are transfixed when he tells them how he could earn £600 per day debt collecting and £3,000 in an afternoon setting up drug deals with his mobile phone; and how he turned his back on it all through the power of God. 'One RE teacher said to me that I'd done in forty-five minutes what he's been trying to do in seven years,' he says.

So how does he approach his work in schools? His expression hardens. 'Youngsters today are hungry for the truth. I think they realise that the world doesn't fulfil them. They are looking for something that is God. But often they don't know it's God. They tend to be told by the world that they are useless and not worth anything. Many are lonely because they put over a false image of themselves and forget who they really are. When Youth 2000 goes into a school we try and raise their self-worth; make them realise that they are special; that God loves them and cherishes them. We say God's not a God of rules and regulations but a God of freedom and joy. Often kids are told they need Nike or Reebok because their name's not good enough, or they need this amount of money. Jesus says you don't need any of it because you are already beautiful; because you're made in my image and I don't make rubbish.'

Despite such a powerful experience of God that night in his flat, John stresses that trying to live the gospel values of Jesus calls for a daily conversion, especially in a world that is driven by materialism and success. 'But I have learnt that God doesn't love us because we are perfect or not love us because we are not perfect. He comes to us in our weaknesses.'

Without daily Mass and a disciplined prayer life he would have nothing to give, he suggests. Since visiting Jerusalem and Bethlehem, and walking in the footsteps of Jesus and the apostles, he has discovered the Bible in a new way. He has also developed a deep devotion to the Virgin Mary, who, observed St Ephraem in the fifth century, is 'the ground in which the Church was sown'.

Reflecting on his life as a hard man, he says with

disdain, 'There's such a romantic myth about the kind of life I led. But there was much self-hatred and pain. You get to the point when you think that you're invincible. I thought people who obeyed the law and did a nine to five job were all being conned. People didn't matter. All that mattered was you. You could be laughing and joking, then beat someone senseless, and then be laughing and joking again. When I was giving a talk to some young offenders one of them asked what was the longest prison sentence you had. I replied twenty-seven years without God. I told them I'm not here wanting you to be pillar of society. I just want you to feel the peace and love I have.'

The Adoptee

'It took me a long time to come eventually to this decision. I can only presume it must be like cohabiting with someone for so long that you think there is no point in getting married,' says James Parker, sitting in his office at Archbishop's House, Westminster.

He is looking back on his reception into the Catholic Church during the 1992 Easter Vigil at St Joseph's, Roehampton, south-west London. 'This couldn't have been further from the truth concerning my reception into the Catholic Church. At the end of the Easter Vigil I felt as though I had at last "come home" and remember bursting into tears, thinking to myself, "Why didn't I do this earlier?"'

Wearing a snazzy navy blue suit and with eyes that immediately lock onto you, thirty-one-year-old James bubbles with enthusiasm when recounting why he became a Catholic. 'For me, two underlying points were a discovery of truth and a place of belonging. Christ is the truth and the Church is the place of belonging,' he fires off, in a voice that would not be out of place on one of those wacky TV pop programmes.

Then, pausing to expand on this statement, he adds, 'In the Catholic Church's tradition I found a place that had an understanding of my journey and the journey of humankind over the centuries. In the teaching I was presented with a vision; a higher calling for my life. To balance this, the Church provided me with a way to follow that spoke of continuing salvation. Inevitably we all fall at some point or other; we all mess up at times, but I came to realise that God's grace – his love and strength – is always available.'

Adopted along with his twin sister at the age of six months by an Anglican couple in Sheffield, two years ago they met their natural mother for the first time. 'This was a very important and significant event in my life journey. As I spent time reflecting on the commandment, "Honour your father and your mother" I became aware that, although I had tried to honour God, my Heavenly Father, and also my parents, I had two other parents I needed to honour. With confidence and peace, and the love and understanding of my adoptive family, my twin and I set about finding our birth mother. Naturally we were apprehensive about how our first meeting would go, but things could not have gone better. We have since met up with numerous uncles, aunts and cousins and continue to keep in touch.' A part of him would still like to track down his Middle Eastern father, he reveals.

After being educated in a mildly evangelical Anglican prep school, at the age of thirteen he went to Mount St Mary's College, a Catholic independent school run by the Jesuits. 'After a time I realised that there was a big difference between my friends at school who were practising Catholic and those who weren't or had no Christian faith at all, he recalls.

Here, he met Fr Patrick Rorke who had a profound effect on him. 'This man was able to love me in areas where I couldn't love myself. He would look right into the depth of me with his eyes full of love and acceptance. I knew God was present in him.'

Although not a Catholic, James one day asked Fr Pat if he would hear his confession. 'In revealing to this godly man the thoughts and actions of my past that weighed heavily on my conscience, he was able to minister to me God's love and forgiveness. I left that room walking on air.

I knew God had heard me and more importantly that he loved me and forgave me for anything I had done wrong in the past.' By sixteen he was regularly attending daily Mass at the school.

His GCSEs and A levels secured him a place to read French and music at what is now the University of Surrey, Roehampton, in London. At the end of his first year he was invited to a Catholic Charismatic prayer group and attended the Life in the Spirit seminars. 'This was a turning point in my life because I made a decision that I wanted God on board in my weakness. I made a decision: God I give you my sin; come and take over. During my student years I attended Anglican, evangelical and house churches. But on reflection, I found that everything the other churches had was in the Catholic Church: the proclamation of the Word, the Eucharist and the understanding of charisms.

'Of course, central to my decision to be received into full communion with the Catholic Church was the Church's teaching on the Eucharist. I had always believed that the fullness of God dwelt in Jesus as a man. Could I explain this? No, and yet I still believed. It wasn't so ridiculous therefore for me to believe that by the act of consecration the whole substance of the bread is changed into the substance of Christ's body and the whole substance of the wine into Christ's blood. I couldn't explain this either and yet I believed. Over a period of time the body and blood, together with the soul and divinity, of Jesus Christ being presented before me in the Eucharist created an overwhelming hunger within me that I knew could not be satisfied anywhere else. I yearned to receive Jesus truly, wholly and substantially present in the Eucharist. To be offered the opportunity to receive him daily at Mass and yet not to pursue this would ultimately have been my denial of him. I had already done this often enough. I knew it was time for me to accept the Catholic Church's teaching and to be adopted into the family that met around the Eucharistic table.'

Spending more time in prayer, he insists, began to transform his life. 'The Church's teaching has always been very clear and at that time my life did not reflect it. I decided to trust that God's unconditional love would give me the strength to live according to the Church's teaching. I asked the Holy Spirit to lead me into what is, and always has been, the truth. My misunderstandings and reckless emotions were challenged, broken and put right.' It was, he admits, a difficult and painful time. 'I was taken on a journey that was nothing less than incredible. I found in God a deeper love than I'd ever found in any relationship, even with my friends or family.'

He has drawn great spiritual insight from meditating on the life of the Virgin Mary. He says, 'She's an example to me of obedience and discipleship. I could certainly relate to her being deeply disturbed at the Annunciation. God suddenly had different plans for her life, better, more satisfying plans, the outcome of which I believe she could never have imagined. When I look back at the pattern my life has taken since I started trusting in God, I can see that the same has been true for me. I have often felt uncomfortable with the Word of God but when I have blindly stepped out to be obedient to his word, then his plans have always outstripped my wildest imaginings. It's so true that God's foolishness is wiser than Man's greatest wisdom.'

Following graduation, he joined a company involved in the management of major international sport and music events, such as Wimbledon. Then in 1993, just a year after he was received into the Church, he was surprised when he was offered an administrative post in the Africa and Middle East section of the Vatican's Evangelisation 2000 office in Rome.

Vatican City, the territorial seat of the papacy, is the smallest state in the world, less than a third the size of London's Hyde Park. Within its limits are museums, art galleries, a radio station, post office, a railway, astronomical observatory, the Vatican Palace, the Basilica of St Peter, and the offices of the Church departments that are responsible for meeting the spiritual and material needs of the world's one billion Catholic population. The Pope occupies a monarchical position and is responsible for 1339 employees, 471 citizens and 314 residents.

'My time in Rome was incredible. The highlight of my stay had to be playing the music early one morning for a Mass with Pope John Paul II in his private chapel. Rome will always remain a very special place for me. And not just because of the vino and pizza!'

James was given the opportunity to travel to numerous countries, including Tanzania, Poland, Egypt, Zimbabwe and South Africa, and gained an insight into the global family of the Church. 'I attended the wedding of an opulent family at midnight in Cairo and I didn't understand a word of what was being said. But I knew what was happening. The same was true the first time I attended Mass in a tiny chapel in the suburbs of Harare in Zimbabwe. The locals sang their way through the Mass in Shona, their mother tongue.

'Although thousands of miles away from my family in England and my friends in Italy I felt completely at home. I was with members of God's family united through the Eucharist, the same Jesus Christ I had received time and time again at Mass in London, in Sheffield and in Rome.'

During this time in the 'Eternal City' he met Mother Teresa on a number of occasions. 'I remember the first time we met each other. It couldn't have been more unplanned. I had been asked to deliver a parcel to one of her convents in Rome. Unwittingly, I entered the convent and attempted to hand over the parcel to one of the sisters. She appeared reluctant to assist me and graciously yet firmly directed me into a small parlour and then closed the door behind me, leaving me there alone. A few minutes later there was a gentle knock at the door and in walked Mother Teresa! I suddenly found myself alone in the company of one of the most beautiful people anyone could ever meet. Her beaming smile, her peaceful presence, her firm handshake and her piercing gaze – these spoke to me of a woman completely other-centred. We talked a while and laughed and then she prayed with me and for me. Only after we parted company did I realise that she had looked upon me as Christ in her midst during our few brief minutes together. Later that night, I recall reflecting how important it is to place every day into God's hands, trusting that He will deal perfectly with the simple and sometimes complex circumstances of our lives.'

After three years based in Rome James returned to England in 1996. Unsure of what he wanted to do, he worked as a parish assistant in Liverpool, a farm manager in Surrey and also spent some time travelling around Australia and southern Africa.

Several years ago, he explains, he sensed in his prayer what he understood to be the Holy Spirit asking him if he was prepared to serve. Having learned that God would not ask him to undertake something beyond his means, he said yes. 'When, how and why were not to be my concern. I had opened myself to the Spirit. He penetrated me and in turn planted a seed,' he says with vigour.

Three years later he had a chance meeting with one of Cardinal Hume's senior staff, who was looking for an assistant to help him manage the day-to-day affairs at Archbishop's House. James submitted his CV and was taken on.

So, what was it like working with Cardinal Hume, one of the holiest people of our time? 'I found myself presented daily with a God-fearing man of profound wisdom. It seemed to me that he had learned to discern the times when it was right to hold back and not to act hastily. Better, this, he believed, than foolishly to attempt to dive into something without first knowing God's will,' he says admiringly.

'Cardinal Hume always said to search for the God of consolation, not the consolation of God. Bearing this in mind, I realised that running after spiritual experiences should never be the Christian focus. By patiently waiting before Him, God met me in the most unusual places and at the most unusual times. There have been times of profound joy and times when I've seriously questioned in the midst of the darkness.'

James sees the Catholic Church as a worldwide family, which, like any family, contains both saints and sinners. Two of its most famous members this century have, for example, been Mother Teresa and Adolf Hitler!

Yet the disciples Jesus chose were a motley bunch: Judas betrayed him, Peter disowned him and Thomas refused to believe in the Resurrection until he had seen the holes in his hands. And you only have to read St Paul's letters to the early Christian communities around the Mediterranean to realise that he was a man who, despite his burning love of God and zeal for spreading the gospel, was very human indeed.

'I've always said that in the Catholic Church is a place least afraid of change where there is both stability and spontaneity. No global organisation has seen more changes take place within it than have transpired in the Catholic Church over the past few decades. The Holy Spirit is forever in the role of renewing the Church, inviting each one of us to entrust our past, present and future into the hands of God who never leaves us or abandons us. I found that the one place that proclaimed the truth, whether I liked it or not, was the Catholic Church,' reflects James, who is now involved, among other things, with running Alpha courses. Taking place in churches up and down the country, Alpha aims to introduce people to the key beliefs of Christianity through a series of talks combined with a meal.

'It's so exciting watching people come to know Jesus Christ. It's also wonderful to see practising Catholics gain a deeper appreciation for the life of the Church and to watch them mature in their relationship with God,' he enthuses.

James explains that, apart from Alpha, he is also assisting with two other important projects in the Catholic

Church: exploring the Catholic Church, an eight-week course which gives both Catholics and non-Catholics an opportunity to learn more about Catholicism; and a series of men's weekends.

'I have met many people who are interested in the Catholic faith but who do not seem to have any desire to become Catholic. There are also Catholics whom I have met who desire to be able to understand and express more clearly what it is they believe. This course tries to meet these needs in a fun and informal setting.'

What's the idea behind the men's retreats? Presumably, it's not about hugging trees and running around in the woods. Is it? He smiles. 'The committee I'm on recognised that there is a growing hunger for God among men in the Catholic Church in the British Isles. Rather than do nothing about this we chose to be proactive in responding to men's spiritual issues by focusing and expending our energies on what we could offer from within the Roman Catholic tradition. Since these weekends started in 1997 five hundred different men have attended. For the many men who attend, these annual few days away are becoming rare occasions when they can take the time to reflect upon or reaffirm their identity as men, not only as members of society but as heads of families and as persons making up the body of Christ. When men are secure in their identity then we believe that marriages will also be strong and healthy, and so in turn will families and society as a whole.'

The weekends, which have been held at the stately Woldingham Park girls school in Surrey, and the famous Jesuit-run Stoneyhurst school in Lancashire, have given birth to a network of small groups that meet each month in Edinburgh, Manchester, Birmingham and other towns and cities, he adds enthusiastically. 'Each group serves as a forum in which we as men can relax together in a safe and confidential setting. Here we have the opportunity to share our joys and difficulties with each other. It is in this small group setting that we are stripped of any masks that we might be wearing and where we can be accountable and vulnerable with one another should we choose to be. It's very much about complementality, and any air of competition that is often present amongst groups of men doesn't find a place here.'

The groups, he continues, provide a place for men to be known 'not by virtue of their wealth but by wealth of their virtues', adding that servant leadership, humility and responsibility are the kind of themes that are discussed.

How, I wonder, do these meetings affect relationships with wives and girlfriends? 'We are watching men make great strides in their communication skills with members of the opposite sex,' he replies, then adds waggishly, 'Not surprisingly there are a number of wives out there who are profoundly encouraged by this.'

As the interview draws to a close, I ask him what he would he say to people who were thinking of becoming a Catholic? 'All I can say is that I found in the Catholic Church an acceptance of the supernatural which goes hand in hand with the natural. The Catholic Church doesn't claim to understand everything. It has a sense of mystery. As a creature I met the creator in the midst of creation and gained an appreciation of all three: myself, those around me and God. I know that what I have received up to now is nothing compared to what I will receive. I can trust in God more than I can trust in myself.'

The Traveller

Telling me about his childhood in Sierra Leone, thirty-seven-year-old Abu Conteh says he doesn't know much about Fr Olivani except that he was a missionary priest, very kind, caring, cheerful and possibly Italian. But the memory of this priest stayed with him throughout his studies in the former Soviet Union and when he decided to move to London, where he was received into the Catholic Church.

I am sitting with him in a council flat in Stamford Hill, north London, one of the capital's most cosmopolitan areas. Walk the short distance to the busy junction with Amhurst Park and you will find Jewish butchers and bakeries, while in the other direction along Stoke Newington High Street you come across Turkish food shops and hairdressers. In between you might easily pass fifty nationalities in the street. Stamford Hill, where all the world seems to have converged, a fitting place to meet a man with such an eclectic set of experiences.

Abu hasn't long finished work at a car park at the Barbican Centre, where he is a supervisor. For someone as well educated as himself operating a yellow and black barrier all day must be rather dull. But he is philosophical about it. He says he simply needs to bring in some money while he completes his studies, which he hopes will launch his career in marketing.

One of five children, he grew up as Muslim in a village

in Sierra Leone, west Africa, before moving when he was eight to the capital, Freetown. In a country where traditional African belief systems still exercise influence and where a sense of the spiritual pervades every aspect of life Abu, unsurprisingly, became interested in religion at an early age.

'My father was not that strict with me. I attended Seventh Day Adventist and Jehovah's Witness meetings during my teenage years and he didn't object, even when we went out knocking on doors for the Witnesses,' he says with a mixture of admiration and gratitude. 'I told him I'm not sure where I want to belong, so I have to look at different beliefs.'

Looking back, he says Islam failed to make an impact on him. 'In Islam if you don't know Arabic you can't understand what is being taught. At school we used to recite the Koran but I didn't know what it meant.'

His two years at a Catholic primary school and the presence of Fr Olivani were to leave a lasting impression on him. 'He liked me, and I remember that the Catholics used to bring oil, corn flour and clothes to us. I wondered what had brought them to this remote part of our country. And I remember that my Catholic friends used to have European sponsors who would pay school fees and send them presents at Christmas.'

Seven years at a Muslim primary school were followed by an Anglican secondary education, where Abu won a scholarship to study in the former Soviet Union, which, with its Communist ideology, was often brutal in its suppression of religion of any sort. He spent seven years in first Odessa and then Moscow, emerging in 1989 with a masters degree in economics.

He clearly enjoyed his time there and shakes his head when I ask if he experienced racism. 'The first two years were really hard but it then became easier and by the end of my course I almost became one of them and was teaching Russian to first year students. During this period I would have considered myself a non-practising Muslim, although I had attended undercover Christian worship in a house in Odessa.

'All along I knew I was going to be a Christian. I remember travelling to East Germany on the train and getting stranded at a railway station in Poland because of problems with my visa. A nun came to my aid. She found a hostel for me and even paid for it,' he says, chuckling even now at his good fortune.

In 1992, with Sierra Leone wracked by civil war, he moved to London, got married to Mary Elizabeth, a Methodist, and began to attend a variety of churches. 'I still couldn't make up my mind which one I should join,' he says recalling the frustration and uncertainty he experienced over the spiritual direction his life should take.

When his daughter Melinda Koine was born he invited the imam from a local mosque to carry out a naming ceremony. 'When he came to the house he asked me if I was praying and going to the mosque and I had to say yes, even though I wasn't,' he grins mischievously.

But the restlessness in him was increasing along with the need to find answers to his spiritual quest. 'I kept asking myself, "Where do I belong?" My mind went back to Fr Olivani and the Catholic mission, so I decided to go to my local Catholic church, St Ignatius in Stamford Hill.

'I asked to see a priest and told him that I wanted to be a Catholic. He arranged for me to attend the RCIA course each Saturday. I was the only non-Christian. Everyone else was a member of another Church. This was an opportunity for me to ask a lot of questions.' He laughs now when he thinks back to his impressions about what Catholics did in church. 'Some people had told me that Catholics worshipped idols and Mary, and others that they didn't preach the Bible.'

He also began attending Mass, which, with his head jumbled with all sorts of ideas about Christianity and religion in general, made little sense to begin with. It was only later that he began to see how this ritual woven around

God's Word, in both the Old and New Testaments, bread, wine, prayer, gestures and symbolism lies at the heart of the Catholic faith, being at the same time a thanksgiving, sacrifice, sacred meal, presence of Christ and expression of the Body of Christ both locally and scattered throughout the world.

'It was a bit hard at first,' he recalls. 'I felt isolated and didn't understand what was going on.' Gradually what he was learning on the RCIA course began to shed light on the Mass. Along with several hundred other catechumens he attended Mass celebrated by Cardinal Hume at Westminster Cathedral.

He was deeply moved by both the experience and the history of the Church reflected in the list of Popes on a plaque on the cathedral wall, the mosaics, chapels devoted to different saints, and the overall grandeur of a church that was built not in European style but in that of ancient Byzantium.

During what he says was an emotional Easter Vigil at St Ignatius in 1999 he and Melinda were both baptised Catholic. 'It's a feeling that's difficult to describe. The church was packed. The Mass was so special. It lasted about three hours but it didn't seem like it. Something extraordinary was happening to me. I remember being asked to stand up while the rest of the congregation were kneeling.'

Abu is currently studying a post-graduate diploma in Management Studies with a view to undertaking an MBA in Marketing Management. He says he hopes to become a catechist in his parish so he can help others grow in the Christian faith.

'Western Europe brought Christianity to Africa, but now it's the other way around,' he notes. 'If you go to churches in some cities in Britain today, you'll see more Africans than Europeans.'

Reflecting on his spiritual pilgrimage which began in an African village and led him to cosmopolitan London via the Ukraine and the former Soviet Union, he spoke of faith in God and life as a Catholic as an ongoing journey not as something that is static. 'The RCIA is just an introduction. It's then up to the individual to find out more about the faith himself.'

The Counsellor

It was not the rucksack but the multi-coloured waistcoat that was the give away. Watching the passengers step off the number 36 bus outside Paddington station, I knew this was Steve Skibniewski Woods. Only a man who had left school with no qualifications, had gone down the coal mines, entered the United Reformed ministry, quit it after a breakdown, opened a second-hand book shop, become a Catholic and then trained as a counsellor, would wear such an unfashionable and individual jacket.

Sitting in a pub round the corner, he explains in a lilting, ponderous Welsh accent that he's come up from Sutton after attending a conference organised by Aid to the Church in Need, the international Catholic agency which supports the persecuted and oppressed Church. He's the regional secretary for south Wales. Glancing at his watch, he points out that his train to Pembrokeshire leaves in an hour and a half and if he misses that he's stuck in London for the night.

Short with slightly spikey hair, fortyish and wearing thin, blue wire-rimmed glasses, he then tells me he also spent eight years as a minister in London, working in Stepney, Bromley-by-Bow, the Isle of Dogs and Bethnal Green. It was a fascinating time for him, he goes on in his understated manner, mixing with so many people from other faiths and cultures as well as the families whose roots ran deep in the East End. With a touch of pride in his voice, he tells me that three-quarters of those who he ministered to didn't attend church.

'The biggest lesson I learned in the East End was an ecumenical one; not just denominationally but also religiously, because I encountered Muslims, Jews and other faiths. It was an exercise in understanding and the need to accept and enjoy differences. Quite often people from other religions would come to me for help. For example, on one occasion I remember an Asian lady banging on my door at midnight, screaming that someone was killing her husband. I found someone to look after my daughter and quickly went with her. In the middle of this concrete jungle of an estate was her husband, lying on the pavement, covered in blood. He'd been coming home late from the mosque – I think it was Ramadan – and some white youths had pounced on him, jumped on his legs and broke them. It was terrible. His daughter was cradling his head in her lap. I felt such a rage against God. And then I thought, he's there in the pain. I feel the spirit of God, of Christ, transcends race, religion.... Does that make sense?'

To find yourself in the thick of the East End after being brought up in what he describes as a 'mini-castle' must have been a difficult transition. Yet, although Steve spent the early years of his childhood in a peel tower in an idyllic village in the Scottish borders and then a luxury flat in Edinburgh, he comes from solid working-class stock, where, as he says, he knew his place. His mother was housekeeper to 'the Brigadier' and 'Lady', a rather eccentric but benevolent couple who treated Steve as a surrogate son. An only child whose father had returned home to Poland because his family were having problems and then found himself unable to come back because of the Iron Curtain, he soon learned to make his own amusements, as only children usually do, which included 'playing with Lady's mink furs.'

It was years later before he discovered the truth about who his natural father was. 'I grew up as Stephen Woods with not an inkling in my mind that I had a Polish father.

However, often I felt as a child and during my teenage years that I wasn't quite British. Eventually when I was thirty my mother told me about him.'

It was an emotionally charged moment when his father finally came to Wales to see him. 'He had a voice like Yul Bryner,' he recalls brimming with affection. His father has since died, but Steve says he feels close to him when he goes to Mass. Having been reunited with his father he discovered that, through his father's marriage in Poland, he has two half-brothers and a half-sister, with whom he is in regular contact. It was because of his Eastern European connections that he decided to get involved with Aid to the Church In Need.

When he was ten years old his mother moved to Wales and got married. She had intended to marry his Polish father but, realising that he was not going to return, she married a Welsh insurance agent who, says Stephen affectionately, became as kind and loving a step-father as he could have hoped for. Having grown up as an only child, he now found himself with a sister. But living in two rooms in Swansea docks was a bit of a shock after his rather grand lifestyle in Scotland.

Up to this point, he'd had a strong but peripatetic Christian upbringing. Baptised into the Episcopalian Church, he attended a Presbyterian church in Edinburgh, and then, when he moved to Swansea, a Baptist church, and a Congregationalist church. He found himself a member of the United Reformed Church when the Congregationalists merged with the Presbyterians in 1972.

'I've never been stuck on denominations,' he says nonchalantly. 'I believe that Christ is greater than the Church; greater than Christianity. But I'm very happy to be Catholic now.'

He developed a brain tumour at fourteen and, as a result, was often absent from school. The future must have looked a little bleak in that summer in 1961 when he walked out of the school gates without any qualifications. He was taken on as an apprentice at a Swansea printing company. But he says, screwing up his face, he hated the five years he spent there. In search of himself, and in an attempt to reconnect with his roots, he packed his suitcase and headed off to the Scottish borders and spent a year working in a spinning mill in Galashiels before returning to Wales.

No doubt intrigued by the stories and myths he had heard about life down the pit, he was taken on as a miner at Brynlliw Colliery when he returned home. The work was hard, he acknowledges, but he enjoyed the camaraderie and spirit that bonded the men together as they hacked and drilled 1200 feet underground. After three years he felt he needed a job that drew more on his emotional than physical side, so he became a care assistant.

By now, he was married and had moved from being a lay preacher to an elder at his local United Reformed church. He was surprised when it was suggested that he go into the full-time ministry. So, after collecting a clutch of O levels at a college of further education, he was accepted by the Memorial College, Swansea, to study for degree in theology. On the morning of the first day at the college his wife had to drive him round the block four times, so nervous was he. He realised he was escaping his working-class background, like the main character in Willy Russel's *Educating Rita*, but wondered whether he would be able to cope with writing essays and reading about obscure points of theology. I suspect he felt a bit of an interloper. Studies weren't easy, but he did well and in 1978 was awarded his degree, and soon after was appointed as the minister to the congregation in the industrial town of Cwmbran, Gwent. Two years later he moved to London with his wife and young daughter. And it was here living in the manse in Stepney, he says in hindsight, that the first steps towards the Catholic Church were taken.

'When I was in Stepney my United Reformed Church building was also the home to an Anglican congregation,

St Augustine's I think it was called. They were taken into the parish of St Dunstan, but because they wanted to keep a certain autonomy they stayed in Stepney. I got on very well with the curates. The worship was high Anglican with lots of incense, and candles. I loved it. Worship in the United Reformed Church was very non-sensual. I was also involved with a mixed Anglican Franciscan community and used to go there on Fridays to give communion. They saw communion more as an "in memory of" than a consecration in the priestly sense.' Then, in a conspiratorial tone he leans forward and confesses that he finds some high Anglicans difficult to cope with. 'They're often more Catholic than the Catholics.'

In 1990 his wife died from a brain haemorrhage. He was since remarried and has three more children from his second wife, whom he met one Sunday morning outside the church in Stepney.

After eight years in the East End he returned to Wales, feeling in need of change and wanting once again to reconnect with his roots. He was appointed as minister in Hook, near Haverfordwest, in Pembrokeshire. Everything was going fine until he noticed changes in how he was feeling and, more worryingly, his behaviour. 'I felt dreadful. I felt everything was running down. I had no energy. I just couldn't cope with the ministry. I couldn't cope with people. I couldn't drive. I was very tired. And it affected my marriage because I was very depressed. Very miserable. Sometimes I felt I was going a little bit potty. And I might have been. I felt I was dying and I was ready for it. I didn't know it was the thyroid. I blamed everybody. My wife told me to get help because she couldn't live like that.'

Eventually, he was diagnosed with an under-active thyroid, for which he is still having treatment today. He had no choice but no quit the ministry. In the state he was in he couldn't function effectively. Looking around for a way of earning a living, he found an empty premises in Haverfordwest and opened a second-hand book shop.

'It was very easy. I just advertised for books, went and collected them, got a premises, made book shelves and set up business. And that gave me a rest for four years. Lots of people who would come in and talk to me about their deepest and innermost problems. Books seem to help people to do that. And, I suppose, that led me to think that counselling would be a good area to work in. I had been to see a counsellor myself, albeit reluctantly, but I felt I would work through my problems in my own way. The shop was a very successful business in every aspect,' he says, then, a smile rippling across his face, he adds, 'except financially.'

When he was forced to close the shop in 1995 he was taken on as a tutor for adults with learning difficulties. Soon after, he enrolled at the University of Swansea to study for the Advanced Certificate in Counselling and then stayed on over the next two years to gain further qualifications in counselling.

After leaving the United Reformed ministry he had attended Quaker meetings for a while, seeking a more meaningful spiritual path. 'I really found it difficult when I left the ministry. I felt I'd lost my identity. It was so bound up with being a minister.'

By this time his wife, who had been brought up as an English Congregationalist, had been received into the Catholic Church. Curious about her new faith, and still searching himself, Stephen then started going to Mass with her.

So what were his first impressions of Mass? He gives one of his characteristic pauses. 'A little bit of fear maybe. Yes. A little bit of feeling like a square peg in a round hole. A little uncertain, not knowing quite what I was doing. In the Catholic Church God speaks through the senses. It was the liturgy I liked, the order and form and rhythm of it. I kept going each week until I began to feel more at home, until eventually I felt I had come home. I found it spiritually fulfilling.'

Despite this feeling of coming home, reconciling some

Catholic doctrines with his non-Conformist mindset wasn't and hasn't been easy. 'Theologically, I've struggled with certain aspects of Catholicism. For example, Mary. Confession. Purgatory. I suppose quite few, really. I'm working through them but the main thing is that I feel in tune with God.' He looks a bit uneasy. 'That sounds a bit trite doesn't it? It's about my spirit reaching out to God's spirit and for me the Catholic Church has got the best way of enabling me to do that. As a United Reformed Church minister I used to wonder what was my purpose. Was it just visiting and taking church services? I mean a priest has a very well defined role with the sacraments. Priesthood is a sacramental function, isn't it? As a Protestant pastor I didn't have that. And maybe I felt I needed that to fulfil me.'

After instruction with the local Catholic priest, a former Baptist, he was received into the Church in 1994. I ask him about how he viewed the idea of Church when he was a minister. Did he see the United Reformed Church as having an equally direct line to the apostles as the Catholic Church?

He nods. 'The Catholic Church goes back to the apostles not only spiritually but physically with apostolic succession. Protestants would see themselves as having a spiritual apostolic succession, probably. Denominations didn't come into it. What was important was the community. And I think this is good and has great value. But for me there has to be a richer sense of the Church.'

So, I press, what about the fact that before the Reformation the Church was united in its acceptance of seven sacraments. It was, after all, mainly political differences that had split Christendom into Catholic and Orthodox. How did he square this with the Bible alone approach in the United Reformed Church? How could he have disregarded 1500 years of tradition and belief?

He replies that he thought the Catholic Church was mistaken and that the Bible didn't support this view of God being mediated through sacraments. 'In fact, I was very anti-Roman Catholic for years. Not in an aggressive way. But somewhere in the back of my mind I felt Catholics had got it quite wrong. One of the stumbling blocks I had with Catholicism was the belief that authority from God came through the Bible and tradition rather than the Bible alone. Now I can see how God does work through tradition as well as through the Scriptures. The New Testament is only the written tradition of the Church.'

While his wife was obviously overjoyed at his decision to become a Catholic, reactions amongst his United Reformed friends and colleagues were, understandably, far from enthusiastic. Surprisingly, the United Reformed Church moderator in Wales was very understanding, seeing his reception into the Catholic Church as part of his spiritual journey. 'One day a chap who was a deacon came into the shop. He said, "I hear you're becoming a Catholic. So why have you given up being a minister? Why have you given up being a Christian?" I said I haven't given up being a Christian. I've become a Catholic. He kept going on about this and in the end I had to ask him to leave. And a friend I went to college with has sent me a lot of anti-Catholic tracts. Cheap and nasty little things. Why Mary weeps and things like that. Ugh.'

But many people were prepared to overlook his decision to embrace Catholicism. He must be the only Catholic who leads Non-Conformist services. 'When I became a Catholic many of the churches I used to preach at still asked me to come back. I take the whole service except for communion. I spoke to my parish priest about it and he wasn't that thrilled. He advised me to talk to the chancellor. The chancellor said, "Well, I haven't heard of this before. But it sounds alright and quite a good idea".'

He's currently working as a counsellor with Pembrokeshire Counselling Service and hopes to commence private practice before long. 'My wife and I decided quite early on that we would both work part-time. She's a health visitor, works three days a week and I work two days a week. We both part-time so we can both look after the children.'

So, I wonder if, given his counselling work, has he always been a deep thinker and an analyser of people's problems? 'Well I do think,' he smiles modestly. 'Whether I'm a deep thinker ... I don't know. Occasionally my thoughts take me deep down. I wouldn't say I'm always a deep thinker by any means. I became a counsellor, I think, because I'd been a minister for twelve years in the United Reformed Church and when I finished I felt very very much at a loose end. Very purposeless. And I missed the pastoral dimension in my life.'

Counselling, of course, has become a boom industry in the last thirty years. Some are a little sceptical about this enthusiasm for what is almost a secular form of Confession. So, what does Steve think the advantages of counselling are? He thinks for a moment 'Well, the style I've got, and the style I will probably always keep, is what we call person-centred. Carl Rogers was the great exponent of this. It means that you listen to the client in a non-judgemental way, create a safe environment and you reflect back what the client has said, so the client sees things that they may not have seen before, about their personality or problem or whatever. It's very rare that I give guidance. It can be a slow method sometimes but I feel it is highly effective because the person is learning about themselves. They're not being told what they should do.'

For him, is there a distinction, then, between simply counselling and Christian counselling? 'I don't bring religion into it one little bit. It's humanistic. I might sound people out to see how they understand things spiritually, or if they do understand things spiritually. If they want to talk about God, fine. But for some people it would be offensive to bring in God.'

Then, as if having just remembered something he wanted to say earlier, he switches subjects and tells me about the time in Hook when a young Catholic dad came to see him. The dad wanted his daughter baptised

Catholic but his wife and her family wanted her baptised in the United Reformed Church. What really impressed Steve was the intensity and passion with which the man talked about baptism. Steve acknowledges that the encounter in many ways was an insignificant one. And yet, for some reason – he doesn't know why – it made a deep impression on him. 'But little things do touch us, don't they,' he suggests reflectively.

The Mother

'If you've not had children, how do you find God?' asks Kate Johnson as she reflects on her spiritual journey and wonders what is the right way to mark her Confirmation next week. 'There are small prompts. Kids are a huge prompt.'

Home is a neat terraced house in a hilly corner of Greenwich, south-east London. Greenwich Park and the vast expanse of Black Heath, with spectacular views across the Thames to Canary Wharf, are just a few minutes' walk away. It's the kind of place many Londoners dream of living in. Close enough to the West End and the City, yet with all these green spaces and arty-crafty shops and markets just down the hill in elegant Greenwich High Street.

A vivacious, petite woman, thirty-eight years of age and with one of those sharp, alert kind of faces many creative people seem to have, she tells me that when you are a convert it's not easy to find people to tell your story to. You're worried, on the one hand, about boring non-Catholics with your enthusiasm, while, on the other hand, with Catholics, you can feel a bit awkward as a convert. But her story isn't really that interesting, she adds depreciatively with a nervous laugh. Her husband Paul, a journalist, is out and her three children have been packed off to bed.

One of seven children she grew up, until the age of eleven, in Ulverston, just south of the Lake District. She says fondly it was a very happy time with a great feeling of freedom, often spending weekends walking amidst the lakes and woods.

Her mother ran things at home and her father worked as an engineer. It was a musical family and from the age of six she went to ballet classes, though more out of keeping an eye on her twin sisters than choice. When the family moved to Huddersfield she began dance lessons and immediately felt this was for her.

Although the Church figures in the landscape of her childhood only as some kind of distant, forbidding place, she was brought up in an environment shaped by what she now sees as Christian values. This was largely due to the personality and convictions of her mother. Her first husband, a Canadian pilot, had been killed in combat during the Second World War.

'She had been brought up in a Baptist or, maybe, the Church of England tradition. I'm not sure which. But I think she really lost faith when her husband died. Although she brought us up with good moral values, to be good, to be kind, to share and to look after the underdog, there was no God. She would sometimes go to a Quaker meeting-house to meditate. She taught us all the Christian values that I hold now, but not to do things to get a reward in Heaven but to do them because it was the right thing to do. She told us to have faith in human beings and nature. Because of the death of her husband and the deaths of all those in the Second World War I don't think she could reconcile this with a loving God. Later in her life, though, she softened and moved from atheism to agnosticism. I remember at the age of nine in junior school when I was asked about God, replying that there was no God. The teacher was shocked. I had been told by my parents that when you died and you were buried that was the end of it.' Studying Graham Greene at A level introduced Kate to Catholicism, yet it failed to capture her imagination, though she remembers finding all the stuff about guilt and redemption interesting.

Inspired by the London Contemporary Dance Theatre workshop she attended during their residency in Wakefield, she went off to Goldsmith's College, London, to study dance and art. After graduation, she returned to Yorkshire and took up a post as an outreach dance worker with the Leeds-based Yorkshire Dance Centre, teaching from three-year-olds to A level students.

In 1982 her younger sister Claire, a twin, died aged just eighteen. 'It was a really sudden thing. She went to school in the day and died that evening at seven o'clock. She came home at lunchtime from school with cramp. Suzy, her twin, had been to the theatre that evening. She came home to find her dead of meningitis. It was awful. She had been really living life to the full.' Her voice fades and then she adds wistfully, 'Death teaches you that if you love someone you should tell them.'

She left Yorkshire to pursue her career as a dance teacher in Swindon and, then, Cambridge. It was there she became pregnant by Paul, whom she had first met through a mutual friend during her student days. They moved to London and after Lotte was born, Kate returned to teaching at Lewisham College. After the birth of her second child. Lilli, she opted to stay at home. She married Paul in 1995, in Sri Lanka 'because they didn't want a church wedding'. She says at that moment it felt as if 'their bloods mingled.'

Two days in 1996 left an unforgettable mark on her. 'I gave birth to Mary, my third daughter, at eleven o'clock on the Tuesday evening, came straight home and then, two days later, I was up in Huddersfield soothing my mum into death. It was a bizarre time, dealing with life one minute and death the next. As my mum was dying the look she gave me was just as if she was passing the baton to me. She looked at me with this huge, huge amount of love. It shot right through my heart. I was if she was saying, "You take this on. This is what's important". She had been in a coma for hours. Through that look I was able to accept her death.'

Her mother's death hit her hard and she took some time really to come to terms with it. And then a miscarriage compounded the sense of loss and put into an even sharper focus the big questions in life. 'We were left at home with the foetus. I phoned the doctor and he said that he would get rid of it, presumably by putting it in the incinerator. I couldn't face this at all. So Paul and I decided to bury it. We didn't know where. We didn't want to bury it in the back garden. We wanted it to be somewhere that was really safe. I didn't believe in God at this point, so I wasn't going to go to the Church. We found ourselves under the shadow of the spire of Our lady Star of the Sea in Greenwich Park. It was a fluky kind of thing. You had the church, the Henry Moore statue, symbolising art, the Observatory to the east and the river to the north. We felt the baby could choose for itself and decide its own believe in a way. It was a spiritual sort of thing. But with the church being there it seemed ... sort of ... I don't know. It just seemed the obvious place to go.' She thinks for a moment. 'That life was there for a reason. You hear of miscarriages all the time and pay no attention to them. Unless you've experienced it yourself you don't understand.'

She found herself regularly walking past Our Lady Star of the Sea, looking at it with a mixture of curiosity, puzzlement and longing. What did Catholics do in there? Could anyone go in? What would people say to her if she went in? Although her husband was a cradle Catholic he didn't practise anymore and they had never discussed Catholicism. It had never come up as an issue. She'd heard some strange things about Catholics over the years. Then one Sunday morning, wanting space to think about all that had happened to her in the last couple of years, she plucked up the courage to slip inside, an act that was, she concedes scary.

'I was unaware of the amount of love in the Church at that point,' she recalls, resting her arms on the edge of the table. 'I had always thought of the Church as something, quite austere. A lot of Catholicism sounds so austere as well as righteous. I was trying to resist all of this. Yet when I walked into the church it was lovely. Given all the prejudices I had, I was quite shocked. They didn't instantly dissolve away but they melted heavily. The sermon was about love. The priest was talking about what had happened to me by my mum's death bed. I was amazed that such wisdom was held by the Church. I knew that my experience wasn't common. So I started attending Mass. And every time I went back I was just hit by the wisdom, the knowledge, the truth and the simplicity I heard. And I just knew that this is what I had been seeking in my life.'

Did anyone speak to you on that first occasion? I ask. 'No and I didn't want contact with anyone. I was anonymous and I shuffled off at the end of the Mass. I did this a few times and even when Fr John stopped me and said, "Oh, you must be visiting," I nodded and went on my way. I didn't want to discuss it. It was too painful. It was hitting such a note of grief. I knew I would burst into tears if I spoke about it to anyone. I just wanted to resolve it myself. But as I went regularly to the church I got used to the faces and began to feel the warmth there and the sense of community.'

At Christmas in 1998 she felt she wanted to introduce herself to Fr John and talk about faith. Unable to contact him by phone, she went to Mass the next Sunday and introduced herself. 'He was brilliant. So human. So normal,' she sparkles.

Fr John visited her at home, where, says Kate, they mainly talked about Paul, an occasional Catholic. 'Paul goes to church every now and again and has a warm spot for the Catholic Church. He was taught by brothers and I think he witnessed a lot of violence. He loves the Church, but says to me? "You haven't seen what I have seen." Two weeks ago we were on holiday in St Tropez and we went into a chapel that contained the preserved body of St Roseline from the fourteenth century. After this, I decided to take Roseline as my confirmation name. I had been trying to think of a name for ages. And I was really interested listening to Paul telling the children about saints and Heaven. He's such a Catholic! Even though he laughs and says, "I'm not a Catholic." I've only discovered this recently and I've known him for seventeen years. I'd always seen him as a lapsed Catholic and I was quite pleased really. He came from a very strong Catholic family and went to church regularly until he went to college. I think he just rebelled. He lost respect for some of the brothers who had been teaching him. I would certainly never force him to come to church with me and the children because he obviously finds it quite painful. He comes sometimes though. I wonder if our children went to a Catholic school whether that would bring back bad memories for him?' She gives a long pause. 'I wonder how he would deal with it?'

'Fr John once gave a fantastic homily about acceptance. He spoke about accepting others and yourself, rather than rejecting. And once you learn to accept you can move forward. And with the children, once you accept them for who they are, you can then enable them to become who they ought to be.'

In 1999 she began instruction with Fr John. So did she have any problems with Catholic doctrine once she had begun to go to Mass regularly? She tells me their discussions were based around the catechism and then scurries off to the kitchen and returns with a copy of what used to be known as *The Penny Catechism*.

I suggest that the Church can be like a parent. It can sometimes be too severe and produce ambiguous feelings in its children. She nods in agreement and adds that Paul has huge respect for Fr John and he enjoys what's happening to them as a family. 'We've had some fantastic spiritual conversations, but that's as far as he wants to take it at the moment. He's a much deeper Catholic than I am. I have a zest and passion for it and want to talk about it. If I don't go to church I actually miss it.'

So, then, what exactly drew her back to that church in

Greenwich? Was it the symbolism? The need for a community? What was it?

'More than anything it was the ... what do you call it? ... the homily,' she replies, struggling for the right word. She smiles cautiously when I joke that she was fortunate finding a priest who could preach a decent homily.

Our conversation is interrupted by the phone ringing. Kate gets up, and cupping the receiver on her shoulder, asks in one of those wife-to-husband voices, 'What are you up to? Okay. See you later.' Then, as a footnote, adds with a chuckle, 'I've got this journalist here. We're talking about God.'

Returning to my question about what first attracted her to Mass, she says enthusiastically that Fr John preached brilliantly. 'It wasn't the Gospel as such that clicked with me. It was just this man talking so much sense. I remember him talking about the importance of love and how it was like a baton you passed on to one another. I thought to myself that I had been so arrogant. This religion had existed for 2000 years, so it's hardly surprising that it has this knowledge and wisdom. Like many people, I has dismissed Christianity up to this point. It's not fashionable in our society. People turn to alternative methods of finding a spirituality.'

Unlike some of her friends, she never dabbled with crystals, astrology, feng shui or any of the other 'New Age' fashions. This was, she insists, because a lot of her spiritual needs were resolved through dance. 'The most enjoyable thing I found about dance was not the performance but the way you discovered things about the universe. When you moved you learned about the forces of gravity ... Sharing space. I felt completely at one with the world around me. Or maybe it was just very creative and fulfilling and I didn't need to search for anything beyond that.'

Her career in dance began to become less important once she had taken on motherhood, she says. 'When you've had children it changes things massively, doesn't it? You see life in a different way. I think they teach you so much about life. As an adult you don't see people for who they are. You often see their status or their appearance, or whatever. Well, you do see their personality. But you don't really understand jealousy, anger or tantrums. All the things that children do when they're little.'

As if on cue, ten-year-old Lotte wanders cagily into the room. 'Oh, Lotte, get your book and go to bed,' smiles Kate good-naturedly. Lotte, glances curiously at me, then at her mum, and obediently disappears, the said book preciously tucked under her arm.

Kate continues with her reflections on parent-child relationships. 'I've learned how to understand bad aspects of behaviour and relate that to adult relationships,' she continues getting into her stride. 'It's easy to rope people off as certain types. You don't really see them as a history. As someone who has a mum and a dad and used to be little and is now grown up. You suddenly see the child in your friends.'

She tells me Lotte had made her first confession today. 'I told her that when she talks to God he will love her and forgive her, like her parents do. I actually believe in a very loving, all embracing God. We're all God's children, whatever faith we are. And he loves all of us. Preparing Lotte for her confession, I tried to encourage her to think about what she had done wrong and what she felt sorry for. Confession helps you to confront what you have done and feel sorrow. It's not a scary thing.'

'I was watching Mary – she's three – trying to do a backward roll. She hasn't got a hope. She's years off doing a backward roll.' Was this in a ballet class? I ask. 'No, just on the bed upstairs,' she laughs. 'But she just had a fantastic attitude even though she had no chance of doing it. And I thought, "Gosh!" That's the attitude you lose as an adult. You worry that people will think you are too ambitious. Or you worry about failing. But the only attitude to have is to say to yourself I want to do this and I'm going to have a really good go at it and keep on trying until I can. It's about faith in the world round you and faith in your own ability; faith that you'll find a resolution. And that's another thing about Catholicism: faith; to have faith in things that seem so ridiculous.'

She turns to her copy of *The Penny Catechism*. 'It's a great book,' she enthuses, flicking through the pages and then repeating the question and answer formula that seems to have gone out of fashion amongst many priests today. '"Why did God make you? God made me to know him, love him and serve him." I remember reading this for the first time and not really getting it. But when Fr John discussed it with me the penny dropped very slowly. He encouraged me to underline anything I didn't understand and then ask him about it. I had a real problem at one point about other religions. I could see how this was working for me and how I was getting a greater understanding of the world around me, the meaning of life, I suppose in a way, and getting closer to God. But what other people from other faiths? Is Catholicism any better? Surely they are all ways to God. We are all God's children. You can have Catholics who might be mean characters and who doesn't do the right thing all the time. And then you have people who don't have a faith but who are the most generous, kind, sharing, understanding people you could meet. What is it that divides people? You can't say that you're Catholic therefore you're better. I do believe that baptism and the forgiveness of original sin is very important, and it's not until you have been baptised that you realise how important. But for the person who's not been baptised, I can't believe they go to hell. I believe that God will look after them; that there will be a happy ending.'

What was it like reading the New Testament for the first time? I ask. 'I think I was ready for it. I had a rough understanding of the basic story through my education at school. I knew how the Bible was divided into the Old and New Testaments. I was familiar with the stories but I had never given them any real thought. I had never made them a part of my life. I'd never seen anything in the Bible that was relevant to my life until recently. And now everything I read has a relevance. I find the Bible really useful in bringing up the children. You have all these manuals telling you what's the right way to do this or that. But the Bible is the best. But who can you say this to? It's so unfashionable. People would think you were bonkers. I find it so clear, so loving, so understanding. I mean the idea of forgiving and forgetting is a brilliant thing; so liberating. When you have children you do forgive and forget and you move forward. As a parent it's easy to harp on about when you did that last time, or that you've done that again.

'On Good Friday some of our neighbours invited us over so that our children could play with theirs. And I had to tell them we would have to leave because it was Good Friday and it was an important day for Catholics. That was a first. I thought here I am and I'm saying I'm Catholic and I'm proud of it. On another occasion I bumped into another mum one Sunday morning. She was taking her children to play football. She asked me where I was going and I replied to church. I knew she wasn't a churchgoer, so I said you'll have to come round for coffee and we'll talk about it, as a joke. And I saw this look in her eyes that said, "Oh my God, she's God squad".'

Why does she think so many people dismiss religion? She gives a thoughtful look and pauses. 'I don't know. I find now I will actually talk openly. I'll begin a sentence "In church on Sunday ..." I'm not embarrassed about it. It's a bit like having children. Before you have children you don't want to talk about them. It's something to do with being conservative; about settling down and not having a life. When you have a child it changes your life instantly. It's about huge love, an understanding about why we're here, the next generation, two people coming together. These are huge issues that you do not consider in your teens or early twenties. The idea of marriage is so old fogeyish. You want independence. But once it happens to you, you understand it.'

Kate acknowledges that in modern Britain talking about

religion or faith can be a turn-off to those who have no interest. However, she knows how people sometimes feel, she admits, as she once opened the door to be confronted by two Mormons with smiles even more immaculate than their suits.

Those of us who have been brought up Catholic, or who have been Catholic for a few years, know that while the Church does have a penitential side, it also moves easily to celebrating the good things of creation. Jesus' first miracle was at the wedding in Cana, where he turned several jars of water into wine so that the festivities could continue. And, when the Catholic Church re-established itself in England and Wales from the middle of the nineteenth century onwards, schools may well have been the priority in the building programme, but, in cities such as London, Liverpool and Birmingham, parish social clubs weren't far behind! Some Evangelicals, though, might view this relationship between the vine, or the hop, and the Church as bordering on the scandalous. Yet Catholicism is incarnational in its essence. True, alcohol can and does wreck lives, but drunk in moderation it is a gift from the God who enfleshed himself and endured all the joys and disappointments of his, often ungrateful, human family.

So, two weeks before on that holiday in the south of France, Kate had been both surprised and intrigued to discover that Chateaux Neuf de Pape, a famous red wine, derived its name from when, in the fourteenth century, Avignon became the seat of the Papacy at a time of political turmoil in Rome. She even found another Papal wine, named after St Peter.

When I raise the subject of prayer, she tells me she likes to pray while walking in the park or across Blackheath. She sees prayer as having a conversation with God and admits she finds formal prayer before meals difficult. She encourages her children to take a similar approach. At the end of Mass they usually light a candle and 'give a thought' to someone. 'I want to encourage my children to say formal prayers. I want them to have a conversation with God, but one that comes naturally. I won't enforce Catholicism on them. I find this way is working. On Friday we all fasted. Lilli gave up cake and custard for Lent. Lotte gave up fizzy drinks. I gave up chocolate. We did those things not because we had to but because ... they are becoming part of the way we live.'

So what about sin, then? 'I have become a better person,' she answers without hesitation. 'When I went to Confession I was disappointed about how few things I'd done wrong. I almost wanted to bump it up a bit! I went into the post office in Lewisham a few months ago with one of my kids to buy some stamps. While I was there, I picked up some envelopes, and then went to the counter to pay. Walking down the street afterwards, I realised I hadn't paid for the envelopes, so I went back. The woman behind the counter thought I was mad. She thought there was some other agenda.' She laughs at the memory of it.

Becoming more serious, she says, yes, she has questioned her motives for becoming a Catholic. Was she using it as a prop? Was she lonely? Why did she do it? 'I found myself resisting it to a certain extent and not wanting to go down that road. But it was just inevitable in the end. I love the church we go to. It's such a friendly, caring community. But I sometimes wonder if I hadn't stumbled across that what would have happened. Would I have become a Catholic? I see myself very much at the beginning of a journey, ignorant and unaware of so much in the Church. I find myself understanding little bits of the Catechism as I go along. Periodically, things you thought were clear become clearer.'

The Undertaker

'I remember a priest I once knew and admired who had gone into Kings College Hospital with liver cancer. I went to see him and he looked up at me from his bed and said, "Barry, I'm afraid. I'm really afraid". But you've got faith, I replied. "Yes, but I'm still afraid", he said. I realised then that no matter how much faith you might have, death is the eternal mystery. We're all afraid of dying. We're all frightened of death. No one's ever prepared for it. No pope, cardinal or priest is without some fear of death,' says Barry Albin Dyer, better known as Barry Albin.

'But I've always seen the body as simply a piece of apparatus,' he continues. 'It would be ridiculous to think that just because a tube goes in the TV the programmes end. They don't. I believe in a soul and that it leaves the body, but not always at the same time. That's why there are so may similarities in the near death experiences people report. They often talk about a white light and a feeling of peace.'

We're sitting in his small office in Bermondsey, south-east London. Through the window can be seen a hideous green air-ventilation shaft built by London Underground for the Jubilee Line. When they first saw it, some locals assumed it was a crematorium. Beyond is Southwark Park and blocks of council flats.

With his trademark dove-white hair, parted down the middle, and glasses, Barry bears a passing resemblance to

PR guru Max Clifford. He still has his Bermondsey accent, though, I suspect, it's been modified a little, deliberately or otherwise, as a result of his movement amongst royalty, tycoons and celebrities, both in the UK and overseas.

F. A. Albin & Sons, founded in Bermondsey 217 years ago, is one of Britain's oldest funeral directors. They have been involved in the funerals of kings and queens, princesses, prime ministers, generals, actors, sport stars, gangsters, lords and ladies, paupers and even pets. Albins provides a still point of continuity with the past. This is well illustrated by the inclusion of a horse-drawn carriage in its fleet of vehicles.

Entering the glass doors of the reception, with its mahogany panelling, green carpet and faint background of Gregorian chant, you are immediately struck by the sense of tradition and pride the company has. Barry, his two sons, his uncle and father, three generations of the family, all in their black suits, stare out at you from a painting by Jane Allison, a portrait painter to the Royals. A framed newspaper cutting from 1933, headlined 'Saint of Bermondsey is Buried', shows a thronging crowd paying their last respects to Canon Munane, the parish priest of the Catholic Church of the Most Holy Trinity, Dockhead, where Barry, after many struggles and questions, was eventually to become a Catholic.

Alongside it is a photo of Barry with his hand gently placed on the arm of the tearful wife of actor Donald Plesance.

'I only ever wanted to be a funeral director if couldn't be a professional footballer. I looked at being a photographer because I was really good it at. I looked at being a policeman. But at the end of the day there was nothing more than I wanted to do than this,' Barry insists.

He's fiercely proud of Bermondsey – he was born up the road in Guy's Hospital – and the almost pastoral, even priestly, role his family have played in the lives of so many in the community. To him, being a funeral director is much more than a business. He's over the moon, I learn, in succeeding in buying the Queen Mother's former limo. This means that the people of Bermondsey can now ride in the Queen Mother's car, he says with a child-like excitement.

Both his parents had been involved in the funeral business. His mother was a cousin of the Albins and his father began life as a funeral director with the Dyers in the East End. Dyers and Albins eventually merged and his mother and father became superintendents to the chapel of rest, living in a flat above. They were, he says, very strict but, equally, very loving. It was his father and Fred Albin who instilled in him both the fear of failure and the almost fanatical need to be a perfectionist. If his staff are wearing grey instead of black socks, or if there's a tiny mark on one of the cars, he'll spot it immediately. 'I couldn't face failure as a child, something both my sons suffer from.'

These early years, being surrounded by images of death and grief, burned deep into his imagination, he recalls thoughtfully. 'It was quite a frightening and lonely childhood. Kids wouldn't come to visit me because I lived at the chapel. I was frightened of death then. But I couldn't admit it. If I'd have done so it would have put so much pressure on my mother and father. I was afraid to be left alone in my room, with or without a light on.'

When his parents moved the short distance to Albin's shop on Jamaica Road he became even more fearful. 'This was even more scary. If I went out, the only way back in was through the shop. It was like something out of Oliver Twist. I was already putting the buttons on the coffins and going out with my Dad to move people who had died. I was doing everything. But to say I was afraid of it was taboo. My parents never talked to me about death. It was just a part of the job we did.'

At Bacon's School, where, like the last four owners of Albins, he became head boy, his father would ask for him to be allowed home early so that he could drive the hearse. And, no, he didn't wear his school uniform, he adds with a smile. He had no driving licence, but since the age of nine he had been backing the Albin vehicles into the garage.

Bermondsey in the fifties and sixties was, like docks anywhere, a tough area. It was the kind of place where Saturday night fights at its numerous pubs dotted around the streets near the river were as much part of life for some as going to church on Sundays was for others. To survive, you had to be able to stand on your own two feet. Being an only child, Barry had no big brother to fall back on. 'I was a tough kid. I fought anybody. I didn't care who it was. I'd have a go. Before long everybody knows you'll have a go and no one wants to pick on you any more. Then you have to control yourself from being a bully, which I'm sure I was some of the time. And still to my shame – and I mean that – I'd have a row. Just like that. I'm forty-seven and my last skirmish was about four weeks ago.' He leaves this sentence hanging seductively and then says, to underline his point, 'I will not give way on a funeral. I'm there to protect the families and, whatever it costs me, I will do it. I'm very stubborn like that.'

You might have thought that given his childhood, the last thing he would want to be was a funeral director. But the fear lessened as he reached his teens, to be replaced with a fascination with the family business and a feeling that this, not football or anything else, was what he wanted to do with his life. 'I realised quite early that I had a gift with people who died. I know it sounds a cliché but I can take the pain out of people's faces. And it's a gift. I can't tell you exactly how I do it. It's just something that came to me,' he explains, absent-mindedly picking up a pen off his desk and running his fingers around it.

Although baptised into the Church of England, the nominal faith of his parents, and being a pupil at a Church of England school, he says, all of this failed to make an impact on him. He had been more drawn to football, which he is still passionate about, and athletics. He played for Crystal Place schoolboys and eventually ended up playing non-league football for local team Fisher Athletic as well as Harrow and Wealdstone and the Polytechnic of Central London. Had he not continued the family's business he reckons he would have made an average third division player. That I find hard to believe. It would be difficult to imagine him being average at anything.

What changed his life dramatically, and planted the seeds of Catholicism, was the death of his mother in 1967 when he was seventeen. 'When she died my father's life stopped ... and then began again. They had the most loving relationship you could imagine. I can't ever remember them spending a night apart. And the thought of my Mum or my Dad having an affair with anyone was never an issue. He was totally devastated when she died. And so was I. Life as we knew it had ended.'

It was the comfort and support offered not by the Church of England vicars but by the local Catholic priests and a Sister of Mercy that really touched him. 'I remember Fr McManus putting his arm on my shoulder and saying, "Dying is just as much a part of life as living. And you've got to live." I've never forgotten those words.'

It was at this point that he really understood bereavement, he says reflectively, his voice becoming almost a whisper. 'I've never allowed myself to believe that bereavement is a common illness. It's a thirteen-month illness in its symptoms. When it happens, there's a numbness and you don't know where you are, then you experience deprivation because you can't have what you want, then you go through a feeling of bewilderment because you think someone's coming home for tea at six, as they have done every night. So you have a numbness, a bewilderment, a deprivation, then you get a tremendous depression when you think that nothing's ever going to be the same again.' He adds that in the thirteenth month, after all the first anniversaries, you begin to live a new life, even though you might not know it at the time.

What happened next was, in a different way, almost as devastating, both for Barry and the family firm. Within two weeks of the funeral his father had remarried.

'He married a woman we knew. She'd been a friend of my mum's. But there had been nothing else to it. Everyone in the family was absolutely astounded. My dad lost his standing in the business and the rest of the family couldn't see their way forward in it. This made life very difficult for us as well.'

How did you feel towards him? 'I didn't turn against him. I just accepted the whole situation because he had said that if I couldn't he'd move away. And I couldn't face that.' He pauses and shakes his head and says with a note of sadness. 'But it changed everything for me.'

At the age of forty Barry, in an attempt at catharsis, wrote a long letter to his father, telling him how he felt about his remarriage, the fear he underwent in his childhood, the lack of interest he displayed in his exploits on the football field, all the things he'd never felt able to say. For someone who doesn't come across as an outwardly emotional man, this must have taken quite a bit of doing.

He brightens as he looks at how things have worked out. 'My dad's seventy now and Joan, the lady he remarried, has never left his side. She's been wonderful. She does everything for him. When I look at her now I love her and I am really glad they are happy. They have now been married longer than my mum and dad.'

With a business studies degree from the former Polytechnic of Central London under his belt, Barry began to learn more about how to run a successful funeral service and pursue his dream of, one day, owning the business. Having found his vocation, he threw himself into the work. He studied in Texas and at the college run by Campbell's, one of the America's most famous firms of funeral directors, whose clients have included Judy Garland and John Lennon. Barry learned fast, picked up new techniques in embalming and developed an eye for the main chance, and F. A. Albin went from strength to strength, launching funeral plans, and securing the franchise to transport bodies between the USA and Europe for Eastern

Airlines and Continental Airlines. He married and had two sons. Living above the shop meant that, although he worked long hours and often late into the night, he could pop in and out to see his children.

One morning in 1980, he was in an embassy in central London doing some business. He declined the usual cup of coffee before he left, but decided to give the porter one of the new fifty-pence pieces, as he hadn't seen one. A short while later over his car radio he froze as a news flash announced that the Iranian Embassy had been seized by terrorists and nineteen hostages taken. Had he stayed for that cup of coffee, then he would have been a hostage, or worse.

'As I left the embassy, I can remember seeing five men walking towards me in the street. But I thought nothing of it. And then I realised that they were on their way to storm the embassy. That fifty-pence piece saved my friend's life because although a bullet had hit him it didn't do the kind of damage it would have done had he not had the fifty-pence piece in his top pocket.'

After five days and the deaths of two hostages SAS soldiers stormed the embassy, killing three of the five gunmen. Within hours of these dramatic scenes, broadcast live on TV, Barry and his father were driving across London in a private ambulance to collect the bodies and take them to the mortuary at the local hospital.

While his reputation as one of Britain's best and most professional funeral directors increased, resulting in radio, TV and newspaper interviews, and various accolades within the industry, nationally and internationally, he found himself thinking about Catholicism again. Over the years, he'd talked to various priests about the faith. Some had drawn him nearer to the Church; others, he grins, further away. Yet the attraction towards Catholicism remained constant.

'I gradually felt a desire to share in Communion. I didn't see Communion as just a re-enactment of the Last Supper. I really saw it as the Body of Christ; a chance to be one with him,' he explains, adding that he found the Church's teaching on issues such as birth control a stumbling block and he didn't want to indoctrinate his children. 'I told a priest about my difficulties. He replied, "Do you think that I agree with everything the Church teaches? I don't and can't. But I realise that Catholicism is available for everyone but you have to find you replace in it. You have to accept what you can. God still accepts you because he can understand what you can't accept."'

He attended weekly instruction but, nevertheless, still found it hard to make the final leap. None of the family were Catholic and his wife wasn't interested in Catholicism at all. In retrospect, he says that his embryonic faith put a strain on the marriage. What's more he was the Chairman of Governors of a Church of England school. Why should he disturb the harmony of his life? However, finally, encouraged by a priest 'to come on board and see where it takes you' he was received into the Church at Dockhead in 1990. What prevented the occasion from being a truly joyous one was the absence in the pews of his family.

'It's been a hard journey for me because it's one that my family never took with me. And that's always difficult. It took me a long time to become a Catholic. I never deny I'm a Catholic and I always make it clear what I believe in. But I only believe in the basics. I have some main teachings that I use in my daily life. The hardest thing in the world and the easiest thing in the world is to put God first every time. In everything I do, I always try to think what's right for that other person I'm dealing with, not just what's right for me.'

The one thing he failed at in his life, he says candidly, was the collapse of his marriage. Like many who are in love with their work, he had failed to notice how his wife was feeling. "We'd had twenty-two very happy years together and never really had an argument. It had been great, watching the kids grow up. Brilliant. But then things started to go wrong. And one of the reasons was because we moved from Bermondsey to Blackheath. One day my wife had told me that throughout our time living above the shop she had had no privacy. And I realised that I had been really selfish. I'd been happy but not thought about her. So within a month I bought a house in Blackheath and we moved there. And it was the worst thing we ever did, even though it was only a few miles away. It changed everything. It changed her, it changed me, it changed the kids. And we ended up divorced. We'd passed all the difficult stages of marriage and I should have passed with flying colours, but I take full responsibility for this failure. I only have myself to blame.'

How does he see his role as a funeral director? He tilts his head back and swivels in the chair. 'It's all things. It's an incredible role. You're many people's doctor. They'll come and ask you about illness because you've been in contact with so many fatal diseases. You're a poor man's solicitor because you have to deal with so many documents about wills, estates, investments and so on. And you're also a bit of a priest. I'm more understanding than a priest is, even though I don't have the theology.'

Funerals, he argues, are an opportunity for the Church to welcome back its lost sheep. 'This is the Catholic Church's chance to do something for people who may not have been to Mass or Confession for years. If you say to God, "I may not have felt I needed you in the past but I need you now," he'll be there. Priests should go back to the wake and let the people see that they're not sitting on pedestals.'

What's more, he adds boldly, if someone wants *My Way* played at a funeral, then they should be allowed to have it, even if it was only after the Mass had ended. To deny people is not to touch their needs. And he has always believed a funeral is about what the family want.

This progressive approach to death and funerals has led Albins to become the only company of funeral directors in Europe to practice cyronics, freezing the body at death. They have only carried out this unusual, some might say bizarre, practice on a few occasions. Barry's face has become a familiar one in some states in the US as a result of it being plastered on giant billboards along the roadside. Cyronics, Barry explains matter of factly, is a belief that the body will come back to life at a later date. 'I had an argument about it a few years ago with a priest. He told me I was going against the Church's teaching. I told him I was unaware of the Church having said anything about cyronics. To me, if people come back to life, then we'll known it's the resurrection. I don't see any difference between cyronics and embalming.'

Despite the demands of running a firm like Albins, which he now owns, and being one of the leading figures in the funeral industry, Barry has found time for other interests. He owns a local newspaper, administers a charity for local people, and is involved with Fisher Athletic football club.

He also sits as a magistrate. It was Southwark and Bermondsey MP, Simon Hughes, who persuaded him to take on this responsibility. And like anything Barry has ever done, he's approached it with the utmost dedication and professionalism, having spent four years passing various legal courses and training assessments.

So, if he believes that one of the biggest sins is to be judgmental, something he freely admits he's as guilty of as the next man, how does he square this with being a magistrate?

'When I sit as a magistrate, I'm not there to judge. When I have someone standing in front of me I just administer the law. Unlike many magistrates, I don't give a ticking off to a person. How can I judge someone? I don't know his reasons for committing a crime. How can I judge them? I can only judge the crime itself, weigh up the evidence given to me and make a judgement on whether that is right or wrong. But having done this, I don't judge the moral character of the person.'

He protests that he'd rather not be a magistrate as it takes him away from the firm. But he feels that he has been given a gift and he has the duty to use it. 'It's almost a sin to be given a gift and not to use it. When I send someone to prison I'm doing it because that person has been found guilty of a crime that society says should be punished. If there was any reasonable doubt in my mind about the person being guilty, then I'd let them off. If I had an ounce of doubt, then I couldn't commit. Having done this, then I lay down sentence within the guidelines given to me.'

He would like to see more people like himself sitting as magistrates. Too many of those on the bench are from a narrow strata of society, he claims. They have little experience of what life is like for many people. 'I'm not naive. I'm out doing funerals on the road. I see misdemeanours every day, drug addicts, I deal with families who are heavily involved in crime. I see everyday life.'

Six months previously he had, as he puts it, 'thrown away a winning lottery ticket.' The world's biggest firm of funeral directors wanted to buy Albins and use the name to set up branches throughout Britain. For this they were prepared to give Barry a huge some of money plus an equally huge salary for the next ten years. He knows many people would gasp at such an offer and say that he was crazy to turn it down. But when you are doing what you have always wanted in life – what you feel is your calling in life – already have a comfortable standard of living, and feel responsible for carrying on a family tradition, no amount of money would tempt a man like Barry to give it all up. It would be like a betrayal, of himself and of his family. Or, to put it another way, it would be like selling your soul.

As the interview draws to a close and Barry rolls his sleeves down and begins to put on his tie to make himself presentable for his next appointment, he adopts a philosophical note. 'On cold, wet days at Leytonstone cemetery when I was sitting in the car with the people I cared about most, and the windscreen wipers were going da-da da-da . . .'. His voice trails off as a mixture of emotion and nostalgia take over. 'This means nothing to you, perhaps, but it's …' He searches for the right word. 'Melancholy. It's about where I belong. Isn't that a strange thing?'